W9-AUE-309

WRITING TO MAKE MONEY:

SHORT PROJECTS

LORIANN OBERLIN, MS

Shore Thing Publishing

❋ ❋ ❋

Writing to Make Money:
Short Projects

ISBN-13: 978-0-9912822-6-5 (eBook)
ISBN-13: 978-0-9912822-7-2 (print)
Copyright © 2018 by Loriann Oberlin

All rights reserved, including the reproduction of this book or portions thereof in any form whatsoever. This includes any reproduction or utilization of this work, in whole or in part in any form, by any electronic, mechanical or other means, now known or hereafter invented, including xerography, photocopying and recording, or in any information storage or retrieval system. For additional information about this book or series or any subsidiary rights, contact Shore Thing Publishing at shorethingpublishing@gmail.com.

This publication is designed to provide accurate and authoritative information in regard to the subject matter covered. It is sold with the understanding that neither the publisher nor the author is engaged in rendering legal, accounting, business, or other professional service, nor are they responsible for any omissions or errors. If you require financial, legal advice or other assistance, seek professional services from people in those fields. No liability is assumed for any damages from the use of information contained herein.

Various names used by companies to distinguish books, software and other products can be claimed as trademarks. Every attempt has been made here to insure their accuracy. Please contact individual companies for complete information regarding trademarks and registration.

Portions of text may have appeared in *Writing for Quick Cash* (American Management Association) © 2003 by Loriann Hoff Oberlin. All rights reverted to the author and have been reprinted with author's permission. All rights reserved.

Cover Design: Twice Click Design

Shore Thing Publishing
Queenstown, Maryland

www.facebook.com/writingtomakemoney

For any questions, comments, or to contact the author, please email shorethingpublishing@gmail.com. The publisher is not responsible for Internet or other content not generated by the book's author or Shore Thing Publishing.

Non-Fiction
by Loriann Oberlin

Overcoming Passive-Aggression
Surviving Separation & Divorce
The Angry Child
Writing for Quick Cash
Working At Home While The Kids Are There, Too
Writing for Money
The Insider's Guide to Pittsburgh
Everything American History Book

Women's Fiction
by Lauren Monroe

Letting Go: Book One of The Maryland Shores
Second Chances: Book Two of The Maryland Shores

DEDICATION

This book is dedicated to all the writers, editors, and readers
who have sustained me over the years. You know who you are!
I am truly thankful for your guidance and support.

ACKNOWLEDGMENTS

Friends, family and fellow writing colleagues all had a hand in helping me to the finish line of this first book in a new series. It's a book I felt committed to, having begun my career sharing with and teaching fellow writers. I feel as if I have truly come full circle all these years later.

Special thanks to my family: Andy for answering my copious Photoshop questions, Alex for being my IT guy and library go-between, and Bob for delicious dinners and patience as I finish "just one more sentence" before joining meals. I will always appreciate "give yourself a break" as a much-needed reminder that there is time to work…and time for fun.

Friends who are a work's ambassadors and social media allies are true assets for any author. I am so grateful for your enthusiasm to help me get out the word, and more importantly, for the encouragement on those not-so-motivated days. To Judy Reveal, thank you again for an eagle eye on editing; to Andy Brown, your covers make my messages come to life. Donna and Martie also offered encouragement on my first primitive draft.

Finally, thank you readers for being on the same learning journey with this book in hand. I couldn't do it without you! ~ Loriann Oberlin, 2018

CONTENTS

INTRODUCTION

W riters park themselves before a keyboard for a variety of reasons. If you are like the multitude of writers I have connected with over decades, you may write because you consider yourself to be creative and you might even recharge or relax as you weave words into a tapestry of thoughts.

Many writers yearn to add value to the world through their skill sets. They feel that their work educates and enlightens. Some wish to see their names in print. For them, the byline or publication credit matters most. These are some, but not all, of the reasons you may wish to create or to write.

Perhaps you need to exert more influence over your workday or work location. Do you have children or others to care for? Do you move frequently because of a military lifestyle, full-time job or a climb up the corporate ladder? This might be the case with your career or your spouse's job. Writing provides a work-at-home career that travels with you and your other priorities. All of these reasons are valid motivators for any writer, yet I have left one until last, when for many writers, it is first priority.

Money. Income. Remuneration for the job—part-time earnings or full-time salary in addition to cold hard cash—earned for the sake of offsetting expenses or affording something special. Perhaps all of these reasons.

Earning money is the motivation I focus upon in this series *Writing to Make Money*. Looking back upon my career, it appears that I've come full-circle. I spent decades plying this craft and earning income through newspaper and magazine work, greeting cards, public relations, advertising and marketing jobs. I taught continuing education courses and consulted with professionals who needed collateral materials written so that they, too, could profit, or in the case of non-profits, help others.

Ultimately, I put my accumulated knowledge into a book, published by Writer's Digest Books in 1995. That along with a subsequent book that Barnes & Noble used in an online workshop developed a healthy following.

Imagine my surprise, pleasant and slightly panicked, when several thousand participants signed up for that bookstore-sponsored seminar. I breathed freely when distance learning made it all quite manageable. Time was at a premium, since I was a student myself, enrolled at Johns Hopkins University in a master's program for clinical counseling.

Right now, you have commitments and obligations, which limit time to learn new approaches. I understand the need for concise reading. My promise is to make this encompassing topic as manageable for you as I can.

While I had enrolled in graduate school to add credentials to my name, I had not originally set out to become a mental health therapist. Yet the program resonated with me. It tapped that core curiosity about human behavior that got its start through my writing. I took additional credits and worked the requisite clinical hours.

This, coupled with a different writing world after a 9/11-induced recession, led me to establish a private practice with two offices in Maryland. It's been very rewarding work. When I have had the opportunity to counsel or coach creative types (artists, writers, designers), I tap into the wisdom from both of my careers.

In this, my third book on writing, you will benefit from decades of writing experience and receive some cognitive-behavioral encouragement that I find creative souls need to set realistic goals, allot time, persevere, withstand rejection, and make careful career choices.

Rather than one long tome with its higher price, this begins a series of books. At least two more will follow this one. The first in the series, the one you're reading here, sets out to inspire and explore profitable paths by tackling shorter projects.

You will read some school-of-hard-knocks lessons and start to think about how to establish yourself, your workspace, and writing life for maximum profit potential. Subsequent titles will steer you into other directions and employment opportunities, with instructions and further marketing tips as these are relevant to those writing pursuits.

To make each book comprehensive and diverse, I'll share the experiences of various writers along with quotes, sage advice, and several anecdotes colleagues have shared with me...now with you. I'll offer a mix of wisdom from household author names you will recognize and ordinary people much like you— people who started out at varying levels of skill and know-how.

Of course, I will insert the steps I would do over again, warn you what to steer clear of, and encourage you to follow any path that worked out exceedingly well.

This series will equip you. You *can* recoup the cost of each book in my series many times over providing that you follow the advice and work hard. If you're up to the journey, let's begin.

— Loriann Oberlin, MS
February 2018

Shore Thing Publishing
PROOF COPY

One

Paths to Different Profits

Do what you love and the money will follow.
— Marsha Sinetar, author

Profit: what a subjective word. Think of a fifty-dollar bill. With it, children, even college students, may feel set for a weekend. Loaded. Momentarily satisfied. Adults with that same bill inside a wallet may feel frustrated and poor.

Income from your writing is much the same. If you write to provide extras in your budget—vacation or holiday gifts, funds for college or retirement, or if your keyboard pursuits keep you from living paycheck to paycheck—that's fine. Your reasons are valid and no less substantial than those who set out to derive the majority of their living from being a wordsmith.

Realistic Expectations

This book is not a get-rich-quick approach to solve financial woes and allow you to dispense with your day job. This is a get-income-flowing-first strategy. There is a tremendous difference between the two. Let me explain the distinctions.

In 2015, BusinessInsider.com published a rags-to-riches story stating that J.K. Rowling conjured her famous Harry Potter characters on a train journey and spent the next six, turbulent years inventing the magical world that would amass her a fortune. Likewise, Erika Mitchell, enthralled with the Twilight series, wrote fan fiction during London tube commutes long before she created, as E.L. James, Ana and Christian in *Fifty Shades of Grey*.

Business Insider also reported that the blockbuster sci-fi movie *The Martian* made its actual debut on Andy Weir's personal blog. The author posted chapters every six to eight weeks. Weir did exhaustive research, especially after chemists alerted him to a few issues in his early drafts. When Weir offered *The Martian* for ninety-nine cents on Amazon, more people purchased the saga than downloaded it for free. Weir admitted to self-doubt in a *Washington Post* interview, perhaps until an agent contacted him, sold the rights to Random House, and soared to the top-selling paperback on the *New York Times* best-selling book list. Adapted to film, it landed in theatres in October 2015.

All of these examples show effort and toil, yet aspiring writers too frequently focus upon the wealthy results of household names. They forget the financial, emotional, and relationship tolls in that ladder climb to stardom. Moving forward, think money, not windfall because many well-published writers started out somewhere similar to where you are right now, often in jobs that involved writing though not as authors. They plodded along, improved at their craft, and made a name for themselves.

Jeanne Marie Laskas, a professor at the University of Pittsburgh, contributes to major magazines and is the *New York Times* best-selling author of *Concussion,* which was also made into a film. Michael Lewis gave up working for Salomon Brothers to become a financial journalist, best-selling non-fiction author, and works as a contributing editor at *Vanity Fair.* Carolyn Hax is a writer who worked at the *Army Times* before joining *The Washington Post* staff. These days she's best known for her advice column syndicated in more than 200 newspapers.

What's in This for You?

While I cannot guarantee fame and fortune—I wish I had that sort of magic—I can attest that for the cost of this series, you will see a return on your investment, likely in one sale. That's a pretty darn good gamble. Keep the humble beginnings I reference throughout this book in mind.

Plenty of people have made money with the approaches I present mixed with their own strategies. Former students of mine have gone on to write for newspapers, magazines, and greeting card companies. Some used the business skills to enhance an existing job and others took on public relations clients to diversify. A reader of my writing, work-at-home books chucked the insecurity of corporate layoffs and formed a communications business. Secretly, her dream had also been to write novels.

Today, due to a strong drive and work ethic, Gail Martin has dozens of novels and non-fiction books circulating as well as her own consulting company called DreamSpinner Communications. Larry Martin, Gail's husband, devotes his substantial energies to the business. Together, they collaborate on projects such as their non-fiction *Fresh Start Success* as well as several novels.

Christine Pisera Naman took my workshop. She sent me her first book *Faces of Hope: Babies Born on 9/11,* inspiration that provided much-needed hope out of a dark day. Christine has gone on to write much more, including a 2017 novel *Christmas Lights.*

MJ Callaway, another student, penned lifestyle books for frantic women as Mary Jo Rulnick. "Loriann's course and books were the foundation to my writing career. Since that class, I've had seven books published traditionally, self-published, and digitally," she said when I reconnected regarding this project. "Writing articles and books opened many doors for me."

MJ's books led to interviews and the opportunity to speak at events and conferences. That's what she does these days with *Sales Success Roadmap: Your GPS to Boost Your Sales,* her latest book. MJ uses it as a calling card at companies even before she books a sales training or keynote speech.

"When I think back, the woman who sat in those classes had a dream of becoming a writer," she admitted. "Today, that dream has been fulfilled."

Achievement is very real and quite possible. What is your dream? When will I hear *your* news of an article sale, a column or a blog you launched, clients you have garnered or a book that you took from idea stage to publication?

Unfold Your Roadmap

Getting to a new, profitable destination often starts with a direction, or sometimes, a dream. Close your eyes and ponder.

Where would you rather be as a writer in six months? In two years? In five? Take as many minutes as you require.

When you have even a few of those answers, quickly commit your ideas to paper or enter them electronically into notes. Do not allow negative self-talk or second-guessing yourself to interfere. By the end of this book or series, you will have the chance to reality-test what you jotted down. I anticipate that you will alter some of these writing goals in ways that may astonish you, especially if you keep an open mind. A closed mind, one too fearful to take a few calculated risks or try a new form of writing, closes off your potential.

The point here is to use creative energies, some you never knew existed, and with that expanded horizon, explore paths, which lead to profit. At times, this may seem like a detour from a long-range goal you have forever held in your mind and heart. Before you dismiss this, know that sometimes new material with exciting opportunities has a way of finding you first.

By sharing anecdotal evidence of successful authors and other types of writers, I hope to encourage your new options. In-depth projects, full-length novels, non-fiction books, memoirs, and screenplays are indeed attainable. The additional paths in this book can lead to quicker profit that will boost not only your bank account but also your self-esteem. That latter boost is crucial if you're just starting out or have been toiling as a writer already.

New Skills & Markets Keep Writers Employed

Another reason for my get-income-flowing-first approach: life shows us the futility of our well-devised plans. Recessions resurface. Industries change. Jobs get swallowed up due to the latest technology. Ask newspaper journalists who wrote prior to 2005. In 2016, the Pew Research Center Newspaper Fact Sheet reported that there were 126 fewer daily newspapers in 2014 than in 2004, a fact also published by *Editor & Publisher.*

After the 2001 terrorist attacks, magazine writers had to adjust. As people read online, magazine and greeting card writers fine-tuned their skills to write for this new habit.

Keep such economic setbacks and cultural shifts in mind but move forward. As a counselor, I so often see people lament and feel stuck. Understanding what career paths and options you have prior to navigating tough times will help you to survive and thrive through those downturns.

Increased options and new bursts of self-confidence allow you to let go of "I should, I must, I ought to" and "I can't because" phrases. With little to lose and everything to gain, your becoming a well-versed writer will provide a layer of insulation if or when markets dampen.

$$$ Validates

In my therapy practice, I often see those who find much reward and self-worth from a profession or employment. Without their work, some wouldn't get out of bed each morning. Unfortunate, but true, depressed mood symptoms decrease as income rises. Higher income may bring different problems, but that is another topic entirely. We live in a money-driven society fueled by the sanctioned cocktail party question "What do you do?"

Those who respond with "I'm a writer" usually field follow-up questions. Writing anything, but especially books, intrigues people. Others become curious about your work. Who wouldn't welcome that cool factor or a bit of extra attention?

As imaginative individuals, we tend not to base judgments solely upon money that ends up in the bank account. We see intrinsic value, contributions, legacies we leave in print. That said, creative vision and self-expression do not pay the rent, utilities and grocery bills. Well, for some, it does. The majority, however, need multiple profit streams unless they have other income.

Any particular writing avenue that seems wise for one person may hold little prospect for another. The part-timer who primarily focuses efforts upon completing a school semester, working at another job, or caring for family could be thrilled by an assignment that pays $50 while another writer's minimum threshold may be $500 or $1500 per assignment.

What you can expect to make from your writing depends upon the avenues you choose, your credentials, the portfolio you amass, and supply and demand. Highly specialized medical, scientific, or technical writers could command more than the generalist, staff writer or gig worker. Before you choose exactly what you wish to commit to or steer clear of, please continue reading.

The Reading Economy

Things shift. Stuff happens. Many established writers began their careers without cellphones, made trips to the library or copy center, and met fans at mall book signings. Inventions that we take for granted—objects those writers did not own—have been a mixed blessing.

While the Internet made research simpler and more efficient, jobs got lost when readers chose online news. Society's obsession with celebrity has also cut into the livelihoods of professional writers whose book proposals may get set aside for the famous person's take on a topic. We live in an era of instant gratification and must-know-now news climate. That has drawbacks.

Today, people read digitally. Even those who profess that they won't give up the physical book in hand often opt for the less expensive digital alternative when they compare price tags. eBooks are a convenient proposition with the inception of tablets and phone apps, which make the need for an actual Kindle or Nook device obsolete. All of this occurred within a ten-year span.

eBooks opened profitable doors to authors who could bring their products to readers without months and years waiting in the slush pile for an agent or acquiring editor. However, in 2015 when Amazon introduced Kindle Unlimited, an all-you-can-consume book buffet, it shifted to a pages-read payment model.

Publishers Weekly has reported that Kindle Unlimited, which hosts inventory of Kindle Direct Publishing (KDP Select) devalues what the customer thinks a book should cost. This reduces earning for authors who earn merely half a cent per page read under this plan. Writers who turned to eBooks for up to seventy percent royalties saw their enthusiasm evaporate, an example of clouds that form in the writing world and economy.

Hope on the Horizon

Bright spots do appear, however. In an article on trends in 2016, *Publishers Weekly* reported that eBooks accounted for roughly twenty-five percent of dollar sales, forty to fifty percent of units and increasing global sales. Nielsen BookScan data showed that adult non-fiction posted the biggest unit gains among major print categories in 2016.

Independent authors, otherwise known as Indie authors, have taken market share from traditional publishers as the stigma of self-publishing disappears. Indie publishing, as I will discuss in the third series book, was once viewed as a writer's last resort. Today, it's a first and wise choice for many in order to retain all rights and earn eBook royalties far exceeding the twelve to seventeen percent they might get from traditional publishing. The Association of American Publishers (AAP) reported the first uptick in eBook sales within the U.S from 2015. Most every category saw a sales increase except for professional titles, per the AAP StatShot report released in September 2017.

How people obtain material also provides hope. Whether you disdain or embrace conglomerates, giants such as Amazon, Apple, Barnes & Noble, and Google introduce readers to most books and many magazines. While mid-size presses have merged with larger publishing houses, the end result opens further distribution channels for existing backlist authors. The Big Five Publishers have seen income dip while small and self-publishing percentages have risen slightly in recent years.

"Indie publishers and self-published authors debate endlessly about whether they should 'go wide' and make their eBooks available on many platforms or whether they should put all of their eggs in Amazon's basket since roughly eighty percent of all sales happen there anyway," says Ron Sauder, an independent publisher with the firm Secant Publishing, LLC. "The Kindle Select model, which requires a ninety-day exclusivity pledge, is attractive because it allows readers to sample new books and new authors without shelling out money upfront."

Sauder feels that eBook publishing remains very price sensitive. Most who enter this world, experiment with a variety of distributors, including Smashwords, Draft2Digital, and BookBaby. "The ongoing competition between different business and digital models testifies to the viability of digital publishing," Sauder added. "Sales will ebb and flow, but it's impossible not to believe we are not in the middle of a major cultural change in how people seek and acquire information."

Publishing opportunities indeed exist, including these online markets as described. That's the hope. However, if writers itch to be published too quickly, scratching that without caution could cause one's bank account to bleed. Greater options require additional scrutiny lest you make ill-informed choices. What works for one writer may not be the best avenue for another's efforts or products.

Keep tabs on the changing publishing landscape by reading *Publisher's Weekly, Library Journal, Writer's Market* and other publications pertinent to the avenues that interest you. I suggest that you make friends of the librarians near you for they are your ticket to reading these industry journals without potentially subscribing to them yourself. A subscription to *Publisher's Weekly,* for instance, cost $230 annually. This book's resource section has a comprehensive list to get you started, and I will offer money-saving tips to key information sources as well.

Road Blocks & Caution Signs

Profiting from your ideas and hard work offers much promise; but beware of scams and businesses that prey upon eager writers who yearn to see print quickly. As the time-honored wisdom goes, if it looks too good to be true, it often is just that.

You'll find some scams in back-of-the-magazine advertising boxed off with a promise to "work at home" or "get published!" Of course, legitimate offers may exist. This series will assist you to become more discerning though ultimately the responsibility is yours to investigate any advertisements or offers you find. Steer clear of vanity publishing, in which writers pay to see their work in print without true control of the process. When asked for money upfront, see this common vanity publishing practice as a red flag. Print-on-demand services take a percentage of a sale after you complete your project. This latter avenue is much safer because others profit alongside your own hard effort and earnings.

Scammers operate outside the boundary of common sense and journalistic ethics. Beware of the content provider or magazine that reaches out to you, asks you to apply to be published, and requires you to send original work (i.e., not customary samples of previously published work). Usually, the deadline looms, with no contract offered, only promises that you may land a sizeable project and paycheck. All red flags to run, not walk, away from.

Use the same skepticism with content mills. These are Internet-based companies that use numerous writers to create content for their reading customers or site users. Most of these freelance exchanges earn a commission by connecting freelance writers to their work. It's a low barrier way to begin but content mills do not provide thoroughfares to steady income. When you do the arithmetic, you will be writing for pennies per word. Pennies. Some writers have likened this to being unpaid spec labor (spec as in speculative articles at first).

Content mills may pay five cents per word but keep 1.5 (thirty percent) while writers net 3.5 (seventy percent). If you attempt to negotiate any better, other writers will be vying for the job at the existing rate. What's more, the fine print in these agreements often states that your submitted writing sample will be scored (a very subjective measure), you will only get paid if the client accepts your work (even after rewrites), and you may not under any circumstances, share contact information or external links to your published piece. You face termination if you violate this covenant. Add in another kicker: you sell all rights to your work.

Numerous revelations exist online penned by those who have traveled the content mill path. Writers have shared their work experiences regarding Constant Content, Upwork, Zerys, and others. For some it's worked out. For others, they lamented the control they gave up to a content mill and the face-planted-in-palm position they found themselves in when they surveyed their trail of numerous rejected articles and sometimes being arbitrarily banned from a platform. Seriously consider whether involvement with entities that herd writers detracts from the ideal client you ultimately wish to covet or court. Yes, it pays to thoroughly research the recipient of your keyboard time. Unfortunately, in this era of solid news vs. illegitimate news, some companies load their sites with salacious content designed to boost clicks in hopes of revenue. Hence, the term: click bait.

Readers become disappointed and the validity for all (purveyor, writer and reader) gets called into question. Writers who have affiliated with such may eventually become embarrassed to see their byline on such sites.

So, where's the benefit? Too quick of a leap may lead to regret. Retain as many rights to your work as you conceivably can. Almost always!

While not all revenue sharing opportunities prove to be scams—there are some reputable companies that compensate writers this way—you have to decide once again where to invest your cognitive and keyboard energies. Often, you are paid per view, which amounts to how many times readers click on your content, so in the end this has the feel of click bait. Should you choose to leave, you cannot take your content with you, and subsequently, lose revenue from future views/readership.

Subsequent chapters and books will explain that qualifier, show you how to establish better rates, negotiate for more money, re-slant and capitalize on your existing research and the material you already have on hand.

You can also self-syndicate articles into non-competing markets. As you channel your enthusiasm, keep reading before you park yourself at your desk and pound out those first money-producing assignments. Further learning here should help you to brainstorm more effectively and carefully think through any ideas or projects that percolate in your mind. Then, you'll be set to sell to reputable editors free from the allure of offers that seize upon your vulnerability to profit at any cost.

Two

Show Me the Money

*There are many paths to the top of the mountain,
but the view is always the same.*
— Chinese Proverb

To profit, you must write for some level of payment. Often when you just start out, rates do not budge, and it's best not to push your luck. Beginning writers have little platform upon which to negotiate fees. Experience and a portfolio of work will later allow you to set appropriate rates—not shockingly high or oddly too low.

When that time arrives, however, how will you determine what rates are fair or can be negotiated? First, consult resources such as *Writer's Market* with its extensive listing "How Much Should I Charge?" This feature has been annually updated and reflects more than a dozen professional organizations, which were surveyed to glean the suggested hourly, per project, by the word and page rates. That chart spans several pages. One side effect of reading: it will likely inspire you to try a market other than the one for which you initially consulted the hefty tome.

Some $$$ Avenues

What markets fit into this get-income-flowing-first strategy? I'll summarize here a few profit possibilities though each will be expanded upon in greater detail throughout this book and series.

Guest Blogging & Features — The key word here is *guest*. Being asked to blog or contribute features may put a smile on your face and income into your bank account only in different ways. Ask upfront if you will be paid. These opportunities may or may not remunerate in cold hard cash. You might see higher call volume or a sales bump. What's more what you write may not be yours any longer; check to see if you maintain rights. Even if an invitation lacks a bank deposit, it pays to do the math. The written promotion on its own could justify the investment of your time and talent upfront if you ultimately generate the revenue as business income. Blogging will be covered in depth in the second book of this series.

Short Non-Fiction — Writing articles and shorter work before books and longer-length projects will turn that blinking cursor into bank deposits and certainly boost your self-esteem. Both forms of validation make this prospect pay off. Chapters that follow will guide you from ideas to creation. This approach has worked for countless writers who learned to write proficiently and prolifically.

Through briefs or what are sometimes called fillers, you can prove yourself to one or more editors at a publication, earn a solid reputation, and receive further assignments from these editors or others you query with proof you have been published.

Greeting Cards & Other Fun Stuff — You've likely reaped benefits from news briefs, personal anecdotes or inspirational stories, jokes, quips, cartoons with captions, recipes, and surely you have sent a greeting card in your lifetime. Have you ever considered such content and how these items come to be published? Subsequent chapters show the benefits of writing for these diverse markets.

Editing & Indexing — Yes, other writers hire writers who can read for accuracy and with insight plus wield a red pen. Those who can create an index for non-fiction works may garner work from other authors, small presses or large ones.

Résumés Writing & Cover Letters — People care immensely about their career trajectory. Put your skills to presenting their work-related and educational history into a document that sells them to a company or organization. You need a knack for action verbs and rephrasing coupled with organizing a lifetime of experience into one concise format. Use the same type of concise language, action verbs, and actually ask for the interview in cover letters that land those meetings.

Personal Correspondence & Marriage Proposals — While one might not think that such important and personal writing would be hired out, it's worth mentioning. Did we ever think that people would hire out closet organization? Pet sitting or frankly pooper scooping? Enough said!

Those who are intuitive and can celebrate life's triumph's such as birth announcements, weddings, and special occasions and/or empathize with someone's heartache, helping with eulogies and sympathy thank you notes will take a difficult task from someone whose load needs to be lifted. As for will-you-marry-me question, it's not as simple as in decades past. Couples craft elaborate engagement events. You had better believe that the words that pop the question need to be stellar ones.

Business Projects — If you can write news releases and marketing material, grant proposals, on-hold messages, technical briefs or instructional data, manuals, and newsletters, these are just a few of the projects that might keep you at the keyboard. Add in business proposal development, scientific or medical writing, which are all specialized skills sets, and your talents may be in great demand.

What's Your $$$ Potential?

Research a starting point and realize that published rates may be conservative numbers. Some writers fully believe that if they accept the first figure offered to them, they have undersold themselves. Consider your experience and what you bring to the project or publication. If you set the pay scale too high, you may snag few assignments. Set the bar too low, and you risk working numerous hours well below minimum wage.

You might get frustrated, tempted to quit. Charging a fair rate enlightens clients that you are a professional, not a clerk. It also gives you the opportunity to do excellent work in order to build higher-paying assignments into your future repertoire.

One other valuable online tool is O*Net OnLine, where you can do an occupation quick search to pull up wage data and employment projections from the U.S. Bureau of Labor Statistics.

Scroll to the bottom with Wages & Employment Trends to see median wages as well as State wages and projected growth. If a yellow sun appears next to the text, it bodes very well for future need. "Bright Outlook" conveys the best job prospects. View the resources later in this book for additional sites.

With magazine and book publishers, beginning writers are wise to write more, negotiate less. Once you've proven your worth or have a hefty trail of clips, you are certainly within your rights to ask for an increase or refuse to settle at the first offer.

Some reading this want to know at the outset about potential income. I did promise to show you the money in this chapter.

According to the Bureau of Labor Statistics, the median annual earnings for salaried writers and authors were $61,240 annually in 2016, up from $60,250 reported in 2015, and a jump from $42,270 in 2000. Technical writers earned about $69,850 annually in 2016.

Sixteen years prior, technical writers earned $47,790. The government online database from which these figures came reports also that projected job growth for them is ten to fourteen percent faster than average. For those general writers and authors, the projected growth through 2026 represents an average rate of five to nine percent.

A part-time freelancer, writing for newspapers and magazines, a few local publications, and taking on a handful of commercial clients, could realistically gross $25,000 to $40,000 (expenses may yield a lower net income). If you put in more hours and hustle even harder with national and trade magazines, book advances and royalties, teaching assignments, and for-profit clients, you could earn between $50,000 to $90,000 annually (less with expenses).

Consider a specialty, such as medical or technical writing, and it's conceivable to earn a six-figure income.

The National Writers Union published a crowd-sourced list of which publications pay freelance writers, how much, complete with emoticons to convey how most writers view the rates. See "Who Pays Writers?" on the organization's website. Generally speaking, the best publication rates reflect $1 or more per word.

Other Pricing Methods

It's wise to research what other writers charge in your area, and what the market will bear. Do this as you network, contact writing organizations, browse writing websites, and go on LinkedIn to ask what others believe are fair rates given your geographic area and years of experience. Often on LinkedIn, you can join a peer group specialized to your writing niche. Several books referenced in these chapters contain rate-setting guidance. The Editorial Freelancers Association (www.the-efa.org) is another professional association with lists and resources to guide your proper pricing.

Another approach: estimate how much money you would like to earn per week. Divide that number by half the number of hours that you can reasonably work. That will be your rate. You use half the number of working hours available to account for marketing and administration. Lastly, assign greater value or a higher rate to some services over others.

Don't overlook what most workers take for granted when they are employees. Add in at least thirty percent higher than what you might think for items such as benefits, vacation, medical, retirement, taxes, and overhead. Quoting a project rate may thwart your income goals because invariably jobs may take longer than you or your clients anticipate. Formulate bids with the phrase "plus or minus ten percent." If you finish under budget, everyone wins.

To prevent low cash flow, writers also ask for a retainer as lawyers do or some payment up front, much like book authors when they receive the first installment of their advance against royalties. In addition, seal your bids within a specific time frame such as "this price good until . . ." or "price quote will apply for work initiated within this fiscal quarter." Write this into your contracts or agreements.

Prospecting Future Income

Once you see your name in print, you're in a better place to specialize and negotiate for more money. Of course, positioning yourself this way depends upon your talent and financial goals. Cast your net wide to as many editors and markets before settling upon only a few. In a lagging economy, it can be financially risky to write for only one or two clients or a handful of select editors. When you continually prospect new sources of income, it renders you less vulnerable in a recession.

Some writers work in public relations, business or technical writing and contribute to online markets. Others wish to work only a few hours each week. They invest little overhead by producing brief content, short inspirational stories for women's magazines, tips and fillers for others. With all of these choices, you control your career, the types of assignments you seek as well as the pay you accept.

Professional organizations such as the Authors Guild and Society for Technical Communicators (STC) aid and protect the rights of working writers. While I researched this book, the Authors Guild home page featured news from *Publisher's Weekly* and the American Booksellers Association; new legislation affecting the copyright office; contests, grants and residencies; upcoming events, advocacy and positions regarding free speech, piracy, the publishing industry, Amazon.com and Google conduct. Net neutrality trended, too. The STC site promoted three-tiered professional certification. After passing a test to demonstrate knowledge of technical communication, and having one's work evaluated at the higher level, this certification would add to a writer's résumé and income.

To keep profits high, I suggest that you keep your name in front of editors even when not on assignment. Offer to meet for coffee or lunch if you're within close proximity or if you travel through the editor's city. Share a relevant online news article that deals with your field, or better yet, celebrate one of your successes or send something you're proud to have had published. Just be careful if you send material from the editor's competing publication. Judge each case on the relationships you have.

Maintaining Regular Cash Flow

Nothing daunts a creative type's enthusiasm like a dry spell, with no income. For ongoing cash flow, invoice clients and follow through on editorial pitches and contracts. If you're offered only a verbal commitment, nothing precludes you from drafting a memo of understanding. Add a line that reads, "I hereby agree to the terms of this letter and agree to be legally bound by it."

Provide a place for the recipient's signature and date. Ask that the letter be returned to you. Scan apps on smartphones and eFax services make immediate, convenient return much more likely rather than days it would take to return by surface mail or the expense of a separate office fax machine.

Carrying client expenses is a ticket into debt. Suggest or insist that clients establish accounts with printers, mail houses, and vendors and that all bills for such services go directly to the client. In the case of nonprofit organizations, this works to their advantage because of their tax-exempt status.

Target those publishers who pay on acceptance rather than on publication. Who wants to wait months, possibly years for a paycheck? If you decide otherwise, focus on subjects you can produce easily or limit your sales to reprint rights. Don't factor this type of income into your budget. Consider it found money. If a pays-on-publication client lets its account payables slide, drop them. I learned this lesson long ago when ninety days after publication, I was still waiting on a check because advertisers hadn't yet paid the publisher. While I felt bad for them, I would have preferred this disclosure upfront. The income mattered and withholding payment signaled a lack of regard for writers.

In 2016, New York City Council passed the Freelance Isn't Free Act, creating penalties for employers who delay or deny payment for freelancers, independent professionals, and those in the gig economy. The Freelancers Union became a driving force in this measure and estimated that these workers contributed a trillion dollars to the national economy in recent years. It took effect in 2017.

This groundbreaking decree established a strict 30-day timeframe within which freelancers would need to be compensated for services, assuring on time and in full payment. It also required written contracts on freelance projects of $800 or more. This Act went so far as to state that freelancers who wage successful litigation against employers breaching these measures would be entitled to double damages as well as attorneys' fees. The bill, seen as the first of its kind in the nation, prohibited employers from retaliating against freelance workers who stand up for their rights. New York Mayor Bill de Blasio signed the bill, and it went into effect in April 2017.

If you encounter a nonpaying client, send a polite, but strongly worded (assertive) letter or fax requesting payment; contact the accounting department; file a claim with a professional organization (it might intervene for members); put the amount into collections; and/or take the matter to court. There will always be writers willing to accept low payment and put up with poor treatment. Mentally reframe your tenure with such editors or clients as limited. You may feel understandably used. If your work saw print, you got a few clips to help you achieve additional assignments from better known, reputable publishers. Learn from it and move to higher income potential.

Negotiating Even More

Keep your marketing efforts alive, and approach dormant clients with proposals for new work, at least semi-annually if not quarterly. With every new assignment, be prepared to negotiate.

If you have asked for better and different rates, list why you feel you deserve more than the typical fee. Be prepared to answer what makes you unique to this assignment. Factor into any discussions who pays for major expenses, what rights you're selling (maintain as many rights as possible), and a kill fee or amount paid if assignment is canceled. At all times, remain client focused in what you bring to the bargaining table. Concentrate on the client's benefit and the value of your services, leaving out your business costs. Sure, you should factor these into your numbers, but silently. If you've established a track record of consistently meeting client/editor needs, demand what you're worth. Sometimes it's wise to set rates and stick to them, particularly for commercial projects.

Be creative in your negotiations so that you might earn a few perks in addition to payment. This helps beginning writers, in particular. If you're writing for a trade association, ask for a free membership. If you could use additional books by the publisher, agree to be paid partly in credit through tangible material.

Reviewers of books, movies, and other entertainment don't usually earn much but get to keep the book or experience an event. Publishers have routinely offered beginners a free magazine subscription in lieu of monetary payment. I'm not advocating working for free copies beyond getting those first one or two published clippings. Get these however you can and decide if your effort is worth low payment beyond that.

New projects open doors to obtain something you didn't have before. Find a middle ground so that you and your editor feel comfortable. When you are in a better position to negotiate, throw out figures ten to fifteen percent higher than what you might ideally like so that you don't undersell yourself.

If you work on retainer, I encourage a written agreement establishing the maximum of hours worked, a price for overtime extended to your clients, and a review period to revisit payment that's mutually agreeable. This protects you from working at the same rate for years on end, and it relieves you of guessing when it would be appropriate to broach the subject of renegotiation. You'll feel more comfortable and be able to discuss money matters from a position of confidence and strength.

Technology Tantamount to Profit

It's rare these days, but I have met writers (okay, usually of an older generation) who eschew technology. They don't have email accounts. If they have a home computer, its parts needed to be recycled ten years ago. You get the picture.

These folks fail to make serious money. While writers don't need to fork out thousands for the latest technology, they do need appropriate hardware, software, and the Internet. They need word processing. Microsoft Office is fairly standard, but if a yearly subscription strains the budget consider Apple's Pages (only on Mac) or the free Libre Office Writer. Thumb drives, the Cloud or some other backup platform are absolutely necessary because your work has monetary value. Lose it and you lose income. Miserly or disorganized behavior begets professional misery.

Careful Records Pay Off

Log your submissions, along with photocopies of cover letters, manuscripts, queries, and other correspondence. This practice will help to delineate your work as a business from which you intend to profit, one test the IRS uses to distinguish a true business entity from a hobby.

Good record keeping reminds you to follow up. A spreadsheet, three-ring binder, and filing system will suit most writers. Use a similar method for recording income, invoices, expenses, car mileage, and computer usage. Record bank deposits with sufficient notation to explain the income if you're ever audited. Smaller publications frequently send checks without a perforated stub. Attach a photocopy to the invoice and note the income in your ledger or spreadsheet.

At the start of each year, write down your beginning automobile mileage as well as the ending miles each year end. Record mileage driven for business appointments. If others use your computer, log your time (for depreciation purposes). Also, be sure to keep receipts of photocopies, subscriptions, software, membership, online bookstore or other purchases, and essentially any item that will lower your taxable income.

When choosing credit cards, either make one exclusively for your business use and/or choose an affinity or reward-focused credit card that can earn you airline miles, cash back, hotel points or some other perk. Many airline cards have dining and shopping portals. For online shopping, simply log in through the portal and connect to a myriad of services and stores. Sign up for weekly email alerts when retailers grant multiple times the reward points. It adds up. Similarly, register the credit card (or others) onto the dining portal, dine or order carry-out food from these establishments, and you end up with additional air mile rewards.

When you write merely for pleasure, records are not as vital. Since you're reading a book with the intent purpose of profit, you'll benefit from further resources regarding IRS guidelines. To pass that sniff test, a business must derive a profit (as opposed to a loss) three out of five years in operation, be run by someone with appropriate knowledge, and have past and likely future success. Generally, any losses taken should be beyond the taxpayer's control, reflect a start-up phase or possibly a new product launch. Consult a Certified Public Accountant (CPA) regarding your individual business and tax circumstances.

Three

Journalism Basics

Let grammar, punctuation, and spelling into your life!
Even the most energetic and wonderful mess
has to be turned into sentences.
— Terry Pratchett, author

M any paths lead to the same direction: higher profit. Yet if your writing lands on an editor's desk or on an electronic device as anything less than clear and concise, rejections will reach you before any bank deposit. In this Internet age, dissatisfied readers will call you out on errors, including spelling and grammar.

Writing like a journalist is not rocket science, nor does it require a four-year journalism degree. I'll get to the particular perks of education because young people can benefit the most from that solid foundation. However, many college graduates cannot write worth a damn, and some people who never took a formal writing class have become best-selling authors.

It's all about what you write. Skill and style make that product a pleasant reading experience.

Journalistic Skills & Style

Tempted to bypass this chapter? Please don't. Despite the discomfort of uncovering deficits, these next few pages may help you to detect remedial work that will enhance your style, thus your income.

People have vast information sources. Every word must count and attract readers, more so today than decades ago. Trimming excessive verbiage—writing tight—has always been a motto. The best prose gets cultivated out of revision. Without a check of spelling, grammar and usage, plus proofreading a document (multiple times), a writer sacrifices the lifeblood of one's work and income.

To write well, you must also possess a wide vocabulary. Often writers rely too heavily upon software tools such as spell check or red (colorful) underlines in one popular program. You should have adequate spelling skills that, at the very least, alert you to consult the dictionary. News flash: there are no flags or underlines for lackluster or redundant word choice. You must consult the thesaurus as a new powerful habit.

To develop a personal style of your own, continually read, write, and absorb how sentence variety and structure flows. Use the search command to find overused phrasing.

English 3200 is a must-have grammar go-to. Yes, it's pricier than some resources. Consider it a gift to self (as well as a business expense), the effects of which will keep giving back to your livelihood. Grammar won't seem as tedious to learn or refresh when you spend fifteen minutes daily using this self-study guide. You will read a question and immediately see feedback as you turn each page. Lessons build upon one another.

Another good book that will help you to distinguish between tough word choices such as dove or dived, insure or ensure, and a myriad of other confounding phrases is *Get A Grip on Your Grammar* by Kris Spisak. Published in 2017, this book contains the differences of online and on-line, login, log-in, or log in, merely to name a few.

Grammarly started as an online grammar checking tool, but with so many of us conducting business, answering important emails and checking documents on our portable devices, it's now an App. I spotted a mention in, why of course, a filler in *The Washington Post.* I downloaded it to my iPhone, and I already see the value when my fingers mean to hit certain characters yet the autocorrect creates something other than I intended.

Haven't we all had to explain ourselves out of an iPhone glitch that had us writing something odd when we thought otherwise?

As you type, the App offers feedback. Tap on the suggestion and you avoid having to correct yourself later.

Degrees of Education

Does a college degree matter? What if it's not in journalism or creative writing? When I taught a freelance class, a student of mine lamented that she should have majored in journalism instead of nursing. I helped her to reframe this assumption—what counselors call automatic thoughts.

As a reader, would you rather take health advice from someone with R.N. credentials or someone with a liberal arts focus? Though journalists do their research, credentials add authority and would surely open editorial doors and give readers a sense of security regarding advice offered.

In professional publications, degrees do make a difference. Editors at peer-reviewed journals and magazines published by professional organizations look for contributors to know and understand the jargon, focus and mission of subscribers or organization members.

Otherwise, a liberal arts background with its variety of general education credits will aid you. When I worked primarily as a freelance writer, I would call upon and interview sources in the arts, business, healthcare, law, retail and restaurants, psychology and relationships, parenting, science and technology. Having a modicum of subject knowledge helps a writer to brainstorm relevant questions, and far beyond that, to query editors with a bit more confidence.

College programs expose you to more than just theory. They give you the opportunity to learn the history of journalism, public relations or whatever your major. As a student, you can take advantage of internships, be on the staff of student publications, or better yet, become an editor of them. Then come the benefits of writing samples and professor recommendations.

All this said, there are always excellent writers whose only degrees are honorary or none at all. You be the judge. This series will show you a broad range of successful writers, some of whom made it to the top without higher education.

Shore Thing Publishing
PROOF COPY

Should You Invest in A Graduate Degree?

Many writers consider a Master of Fine Arts (M.F.A.) to be their terminal degree; yet for university teaching, it's the Ph.D. In artistic fields, you are typically judged far more on the body of your work than on credentials you hold.

The competition in some M.F.A. programs can be brutal. If 150 students vie for one or two scholarships, the careful criticism hoped for in class could turn into tension. Add in the cost (and debt) of a graduate degree. There are tax breaks that you may reap the benefit of, including scholarships, and investment opportunities (such as 529 programs) to finance education and provide tax deductions.

Some degree programs guarantee you more payback than others. Sadly, advertising, public relations, and writing jobs tend to suffer most if the economy tanks. Weigh your decisions against the potential of future paychecks. If another degree expands employment or the added knowledge confers better assignments and book advances, then go for it. The more skill sets you acquire, the more options you will have in writing and throughout life.

Basics: Five Ws and the H

Who, what, when, where, why, and how—essential questions in journalism—give your reader a clear grasp of information. Leave one out, and you will cause a certain amount of chaos.

Imagine yourself listening to your radio. Music creates ambiance while you cook dinner, wash the car, or sit down at work. The disc jockey reads an urgent weather bulletin for "the following counties." Only if she leaves your county off the list and a flood or high winds affect your property, suddenly it matters. It might cost you mightily in storm damage and repairs, loss of property, or worst case, injury or loss of life. If the writer mistakenly added an extra area, those people may have evacuated or ratcheted their anxiety unnecessarily.

Without essential facts, communication fails. The writer's job is to make life easier on people, not harder. So, remember the five Ws and the H.

With this topic, I add a sixth W representing "Who cares?" There must be an audience. It should ideally consist of more than a private friend/family fan base. Without a sufficient group who cares about the topic your carefully crafted words are not going to sell. That's our purpose: to generate income. If few people care, rework your topic.

Interviewing: A Search for Answers

How do you extract answers to these basic questions from key resources? First, research to ensure that you have indeed insightful questions. Always prepare ahead. Going into an interview unprepared is the equivalent of applying for your passport without your birth certificate. It's not going to go well.

The more you do your homework, the more you will be invited back. If you waste a subject's time, as well as your own, it will reflect poorly upon you, limiting future income.

Interviews bring real, live people and substance to writing. While writers may have a broad base of knowledge, their work requires broad insights, perceptions, reactions, and feelings that guide them, ultimately their readers, through unfamiliar territory. Good writing thrives on diversity and vast experiences. Readers enjoy other people's opinions, the drama that recollections conjure, and the word pictures they create for us.

Interviewing becomes an essential skill, whether conducted in person, by telephone, or via mail/e-mail/fax combination. Nothing replaces the ease of e-mail, which eliminates telephone tag, personal inconvenience, and travel expense. If you're paid one hundred dollars to write a story, traveling across town or even twenty minutes eats into your income.

Use technology to your advantage with Apps such as Skype, Facetime, GoToMeeting, or VSee. These allow you to gain non-verbal communication, which especially helps when establishing follow-up questions. Sitting down face-to-face is best though.

Read widely and listen to good newscasts to find the right authorities for your projects. Internet searches along with professional organizations and membership directories can uncover just the right name also. Keep a file of possible resources for interviews. If you're still at a loss for reputable sources, try a public relations website such as www.prnewswire.com and www.profnetconnect.com that connects journalists with experts.

This Isn't Watergate

Most of your interviews will be on the record so that you can directly quote the subject you question for facts and insight. Occasionally, you'll encounter someone who only wants to help as an anonymous background source, more off the record and with nothing attributed.

If this is the case, and you have both agreed upon this ahead of time, then you must honor the ground rules established. Of course, you must determine if your editor agrees. Such sources might be paraphrased and may simply aid in your knowledge of a particular subject. This is the stuff of which "high-ranking official," "source close to the company," or "veteran observer of the field" is made.

During my book research, the movie based upon *Mark Felt: The Man Who Brought Down the White House* hit theaters and subsequently the rental market. Mark Felt confirmed information for Bob Woodward, encouraged him to follow the money trail of the Watergate burglaries, and insisted that he be kept out of the story, with clandestine meetings. Editors deemed this to be on deep background.

Unattributed sources may deem your work less credible. Always fact-check whatever any source, but especially an anonymous one, has provided you. If you do not, you run the risk that your interviewee has a grudge to settle and uses your article as a platform. Any accusation or charge that lands in your story could face legal or other repercussions; therefore, aim to go on the record.

Whistleblowing journalism as in Watergate comes around rarely. Chances are good you will never have to encounter such ethical challenge of this proportion. However, it can happen in ordinary feature writing. It did to me.

Long before I understood the complexities of informed consent and privacy laws as a therapist, my writing had begun to veer into the psychosocial realm. I pitched a health feature on panic disorder to a major women's magazine. The format of the column called for a person's true-life story.

I had a woman willing to share just how anxious she got having to drive across the Chesapeake Bay Bridge, but she was afraid that if her employer read about this, it would jeopardize her job. I asked the editor if we could use another name in the article, designating that it was substituted for privacy.

The request got denied. I didn't finish the pitch, and therefore, didn't write the story. While I understood both sides of this, I honestly think there are times editors would be wise to have some flexibility. Publishers have long shielded minors and sexual assault victims. I think this might best be determined on a case-by-case basis.

The Interview Itself

Before the first question leaves your lips in any interview, make sure it's a question with an answer you could not retrieve on your own. For instance, asking an expert where she obtained her education wastes your time and hers if an online biography contains this. Don't spend the precious moments with your interviewee seeking answers to questions you could have obtained elsewhere.

If stymied for information, make friends with your librarian. Even at a distance, many county libraries have a reference desk where a librarian can look up brief items. If your library doesn't stock the resources you need, request them through interlibrary loan or use a much larger library.

Ask your subject if you may record the interview; doing otherwise is illegal not to mention just plain rude and wrong. I would still advise that you take even minimal notes in case technology fails. Keep these for an adequate period of time so that subjects cannot claim that you misquoted them.

Save probing questions for the middle of the interview after you have developed rapport with easier ones. If you wait until the end, your time may be cut short. Unless you want yes or no answers, ask open-ended questions beginning with "how" or "what" in order to probe deeper.

For two decades, I used "why" as a typical journalistic question. Once I entered Johns Hopkins University, my first counseling course made me rethink its value and shift to alternatives. "Why" frequently puts people into defense mode. A similar inherent risk exists when you as interviewer begin a sentence with "you." Therefore, try to steer clear of "why and "you" as openers.

If subjects stop short of a complete answer, ask them to expand upon the last answer or cite specific examples. When you cover controversial, sensitive subject matter, lead with, "Critics charge . . ." or "It's been said . . ." Though indirect, such phrasing softens your startup. So, too, does prefacing a straightforward and tough question with praise or leading in with "let's say that…" or "look at the matter another way."

Gleaning the Best Interview Material

The mere presence of quotation marks tells readers to take notice. Very simply, quotations have undeniable power. When you take notes or transcribe your interview, you might wish to place an asterisk near a remarkable quotation.

Never place inside quotation marks something that fails to engage a person's curiosity; for example, not a nurse saying, "I'm going to take your blood pressure" that conveys nothing new. Quote what forces interest. "Oh my, I'd better get the doctor" would leave the reader wanting to know more.

When you quote a resource, always try to put your source in the best possible light. Unless including an error in language serves a purpose—that is, when quoting young children or the uneducated—I would mend minor mistakes in grammar or syntax. Don't relinquish control to your interviewees with extremely long, quoted passages. At the very least, attribute thoughts to someone midway. Don't let the reader wait until six sentences to find out who owns the words or theories.

Beginners rack their minds to replace "said" or "says" with substitutes; they will have people exclaim or shout or use verbs that are not even affiliated with a speaking action. Do not. Especially in non-fiction, it comes across as nonsensical. Our eyes and ears overlook "said" or "says."

While your subject may use a too-familiar phrase, this likely won't be best. Quotation marks do not legitimize overused expressions. Also, don't repeat in narrative what your source said in a quote. One or the other, but both proves to be redundant.

The caution you employ to insure your interviewee comes across well also extends to the subject matter. Have you ever read non-opinion articles that left you wondering whether the author held a grudge or wrote with the intent to rant or rehash—worse yet, to sling arrows or wield a political ax?

Too much vitriol looks one-sided. Since people often comment upon online content, readers who ascertain bias may call you out. We know that Tweets and Facebook posts can unleash brutal feedback, which is not the attention you want to attract to your writing. Thus, aim for balance.

After your interview, thank your interviewee, always request permission before using quotes in another story, and discuss this possibility ahead of time. Certainly, recheck the accuracy of spellings and actual remarks, especially if they are confusing or controversial, foreign or simply uncommon. Request all forms of contact information, including phone and email addresses that are regularly logged into. Transcribe or fill in your notes as soon as possible and know that major publications will fact-check your copy against what your sources say. Forget fudging it, going with unconfirmed material, or using biased sources. A fact checker may call your sources.

To Grant That Sneak Peak...Or Not

Occasionally an interviewee will ask to look at your article before you submit it. Reporters work uncensored, free of such constraints. Doubts to the copy's accuracy or legal ramifications might be exceptions to this.

If you do not abide by this guideline, sources may change their recollections. Besides, giving this kind of advantage to one source, gives that person unfair insight into information that your other sources trusted would stay with you (or your editor) until your article saw print.

Inverted Pyramid Style

Picture an upside-down triangle, an inverted pyramid. Your most important information—who, what, when, where, why and how—belongs in the beginning or widest part of your story. With details contained in your lead, readers develop interest; if not, they may well do something else or reach for the remote control.

A lead sentence or paragraph creates a mood. It says to your reader, "You're going to smile while you read this," "Get the box of tissues ready," or "When you put this down, you'll feel compelled to act." Whatever the result, your lead grabs your reader and sets a foundation for what follows.

Newspaper writing uses the inverted pyramid more often than magazine formats because newspaper editors fit copy into prescribed column inches that could be drastically reduced on a heavy news day. An editor may need to reduce your words, no matter how carefully crafted, from the bottom up if breaking news demands coverage and space.

Magazine articles tend to fill prescribed pages or portions of pages, not column inches. While the inverted pyramid style may work, it's not as much of a mandate in magazines.

Active Writing Sustains Reader Attention

Think about how the following sentence sits with you: "The environmental bill was endorsed by members of both the state legislature and advocacy groups of various organizations who first initiated it, and the bill passed yesterday."

Now, read this one: "The state legislature yesterday passed an environmental bill, which advocacy groups endorsed."

The first take on this contains superfluous detail whereas the second strikes most as more powerful, shorter, and easier to understand. It cuts to the action.

Does your writing skip or saunter along? Do your words evoke images so that readers can see and believe instead of merely read and trust? Action is power. Engaging verbs incite readers to visualize, think, and even question. Active voice, crisp and clear, sells manuscripts. Passive verbs—is, are, was, were, been—weaken prose. Your active writing may sprint the reader along; passive voice stops it in its tracks.

Passive voice disappoints. Your bank account will do likewise if you don't reconstruct limp, lifeless prose so that subjects act.

Admittedly, action verbs show up more often in creative non-fiction, but they have a place in most finished written products. How is it that legal writing gets away with passive voice? Think about it: lawyers defend actions, rarely admit to them. A passive style couches taking responsibility.

Leave the passive voice alone if eliminating it risks sabotaging the beauty of original content. Abraham Lincoln's Gettysburg Address becomes an exception to the rule. Famous literary or

Biblical passages do also. If you choose to maintain the integrity of writing rather than sacrifice the beauty for newer, trendier words, feel relieved. However, set your overall goal to have more active sentences than passive ones whenever possible. When in doubt, jot down that ratio. It will guide you.

Style Priorities

Stephen King's memoir titled *On Writing* urges writers to patrol their prose for empty words or needless phrases tacked at the end. Did you catch what I slipped in there…at the end? That sentence would have been strong if it ended with "needless phrases."

King advises us to steer clear of adverbs and modifiers as well as dead wood, words such as "very," "hopefully," "extremely," or "for all intents and purposes," among others. Strike these to write tight.

Your projects guide your style guide purchase of Associated Press (for news), American Psychological Association (otherwise known as APA, for researchers, psychologists, or other behavioral sciences), or the *Chicago Manual of Style* (for scholars, editors, and publishers). Don't presume to know what an editor will use.

Always ask for that recommendation and consult writer's guidelines, freely made available on many publication websites, sometimes in magazines devoted to writing. These might also be a simple Google search away.

Start your writing with a lead that creates mood, grab's the reader's attention and promises to deliver new information, something useful and full of value, excitement, controversy, and maybe even fun. Your lead creates a first impression. Establish from word one that you—not your quoted subject—control the content flow. Your conclusion may be the better place to let an expert or authority have the last word. The same goes for question leads.

Beginning writers, lacking self-confidence, may turn the reins over too quickly to these devices. Exceptions exist but should not be used as cop-outs for creativity. Work a little harder if you must. Resist going the easy route.

Breaking or highly relevant news requires a direct lead whereas softer news (features) may allow you to delay the facts as you have fun weaving words, taking time to get to the point, with the allure of suspense. Use the standards of good writing style and journalism to create what's in the middle. Much of this chapter helps you in this regard.

When it comes time to conclude, restate what readers need to know and trust your instincts that your ending feels right. Many times, you'll want to give readers room to reflect upon what they have just read. End with the best material you can muster to achieve that satisfaction.

Appeal to People's Senses

If the active voice makes your style more immediate and forceful, words that evoke the senses—taste, touch, sight, smell and sound—invite your readers to experience what you describe through words far more personally and with tons more emotional impact than mere adjectives.

First Attempt: An assistant knocked on a closed office door, interrupting a lunch meeting, saying a car alarm went off and police were in the parking lot, now in our building. Trevor, Wade, Betsy, Noah and I drew scared, not knowing what to do.

Second Attempt with Sensory Detail:

A wailing siren had distracted our meeting enough, but when Gretchen pounded on the conference room door, everyone around the table stiffened. Trevor chomped down on a thick slice of garlic toast. A pen thudded onto the wood surface while Betsy's Gatorade tumbled on its side.

"Three cops just shattered a car window in the parking lot," Gretchen spit out as she stepped inside. "Four more just barged past reception with guns drawn."

"A drug bust?" one person asked.

"Active shooter," Noah mumbled before he leapt and pushed the long, massive piece of furniture against the door. Orange liquid began its slow obliteration of our entire morning's work.

If I hadn't shoved Gretchen's slender frame aside, the table would have impaled her. "We're not gonna die," Noah declared. "Move that credenza out!"

Trevor and Wade muscled it from the wall and motioned for us to duck behind it. As we crouched to the dusty carpet, I let out a sneeze that morphed into a sob.

Trevor's five fat fingers stifled me, and the garlic gagged me into silence. Baked ziti and marinara sauce wafted from the large metal take-out container atop the credenza. Only our hunger escaped through heavy breathing and clenched jaws. All we could do was huddle, hope…and pray.

Can you picture yourself among the office crew in the second example, hoping to be spared? Did you sit up to take notice or skip even half a second of a breath? Visceral reactions count.

You probably don't feel the severity in the first attempt. The words didn't evoke the sensations that might have made you feel you were cowering right along with them behind the credenza.

Thanks to the mindfulness movement, many take the time to experience more, noticing how they feel and what's happening around them and their space. Sensory detail isn't the sole possession of fiction or poetry. It exists in creative non-fiction. Sometimes you can find it in news and feature reporting, even though hard news has its priorities and straightforward style.

You can certainly bring your reader into another world in blog posts, and especially in short works that deal with sentiment such as greeting cards, correspondence, and marriage proposals.

While you may not add this level of intensity into your first draft, carefully consider how you can engage a reader's interest by writing to the five senses as you revise your manuscripts. There's no doubt doing so will enhance your finished product.

Edit Out Offensive Phrasing

There's sensory and then there's sensitivity.

Remember that in today's world, a diverse business climate filled with global cultures and ethnicities as well as the multicultural society in which we interact daily, that we must write to the masses. In addition, gender, disability, and poverty must be respected when we communicate. It's wise to edit out anything even remotely insensitive as you scrutinize your writing.

Fiction has its own set of rules since authors write how a character would come across. There's much more literary license applied. In novels, when you write an antagonist, for instance, you might use insensitive language that's off-putting or slurs that cause the reader to raise an eyebrow and take notice, albeit negative notice. Novelists write in order to give the reader the true essence of characters—good, bad, or indifferent. I will tackle this topic again in a subsequent book on books and novels.

However, this section regarding sensitivity and writing inclusively, for a wide range of readers, applies to non-fiction.

Most of us do not ever purposely set out to make errors that offend, but if you insult any group with offensive words—even if you do not deem them that way—it signals a lack of professionalism. Your editor will be on guard, and your bank account may suffer with lack of assignments and deposits.

Find alternatives to words such as "businessman," "fireman," "salesman," and "watchman." Flight attendants assist airline passengers, not stewardesses. There is no need to call out a "lady judge" nor make assumptions that guests and their wives attend business events. Let's say spouses, or better yet, partners to cover everyone. A woman or person with an actual first/last name and title runs a company or for higher office, not a "female candidate."

Political correctness counts. The English language doesn't have a third person, singular, gender-neutral pronoun for a person. It, as a solo word, can stand in for objects but not for people. Thus, we must strive a bit harder to write properly.

Eliminate male-only references by rewriting sentences in the plural, whenever you can replace "he" with the second-person "you," or substitute the first-person plural "we/us/our" instead of "he/him/his. For example, "Writers must avoid sexist language whenever they can" instead of "a writer must avoid sexist language whenever he or she can."

Lastly, writers need to truly think about everyone who may read their work. Weed out unnecessary labels or references to race, religion, or culture. Watch how you describe physical limitations or mental illness. Terms such as "crippled" or "mentally retarded" have been replaced with compassionate alternatives or mere fact, as in "intellectual disability."

Don't be influenced by years of jokes about crazies, bipolar people, as well as borderlines. Instead, convey the crazy actions. We write about people, not disorders.

Describe a self-absorbed person's entitlement, demeaning others, name dropping, or self-aggrandizement. That shows so much more than slapping the narcissist label onto someone, even when you are writing a fictional character.

There's good reason that the adage show, don't tell applies to writers of all kinds, including non-fiction reporters and other types of writers. Dialogue or quotes as well as behavior remain the primary ways to highlight what people do without unnecessary verbiage.

But back to mental health descriptions for a moment. If you want to display true class and correctness, write "a person suffering from bipolar disorder," or a person "manifesting borderline traits," or his behavior was "reminiscent of those with a personality disorder."

Remember, since licensed clinicians are trained not to use diagnostic nomenclature haphazardly, certainly laypeople or journalists ought not to either. In fact, it could become a legal issue if it's found libelous. Thus, stick with behavioral description to be accurate…and safe.

Good Writing = Revision

Revision creates the best, most entertaining writing that readers share with others and remember throughout careers or lives. For that reason and more, learn to edit your work. Multiple times.

Pay close attention to technical matters (grammar, spelling, and punctuation), content (fact checking and style), as well as any insensitive language that may offend a reader.

This chapter has provided a rendition of Journalism 101. For areas you identify as weaknesses, work on them. To conclude, use this checklist to ensure that your work is editor-ready:

- Does your lead grab readers' attention and force them to remain with you?
- Have you included important elements up front?
- Is your message clear, concise, and correct?
- Does it sound conversational when read aloud?

- Do your verbs shout action? Or limp along in the passive voice?
- Are your sentences diverse in format without "subject, verb; subject, verb?"
- Do you vary your sentences in length?
- Have you eliminated unnecessary phrases, offending or overused words?
- Did you paint word pictures for readers to evoke images?
- Does quoted material sound natural if read aloud?
- Have you used quotation marks only to turn heads?
- Does the conclusion wind down and contain a sense of closure?
- Do you need the support of software or Apps to help with spelling, grammar, or sentence structure? If so, highlight the recommendations offered in this chapter and/or consult the end of this book for a few additional resources.

Four

Bank-Boosting, Brief Work

A little progress each day adds up to big results.
— Author Unknown

When clients end up in my counseling practice, or writers reach out for advice, they often feel stuck, in life or their livelihoods. Indeed, having more options than too few opens doors and it provides much-needed hope.

Since this book has already established valid reasons why people write and has declared its profitable mission, you, as the reader, have choices. Earning cash quickly is one potential avenue, and in my opinion, a great place to begin.

If you have previously committed your days to writing that has not paid off as well as you would like, I hope that this chapter empowers you to incorporate some additional ideas. Examples I provide should clarify how a few quicker cash prospects boost both your self-esteem along with your bank account.

Why Small Projects?

Let's pretend you have only one hour daily, and you give yourself weekends off. Alternatively, if you only have weekends, then let's say you work five hours on Saturday.

You could spend each hour crafting a query letter. You could type it, revise it, have it printed and put into surface mail, email it to an editor, or submit it as content on a publication's website. By week's end, you will have one prospect toward acceptance. Write even more prolifically— you surely will in time—and this increases your prospects.

If your goal is to write non-fiction books, novels, or screenplays, you could spend one week researching material and writing an entire chapter, scene, or perhaps a proposal for a non-fiction book. If you are new at this, you must send more sample chapters than if you are previously published.

Editors make decisions based upon a finished product or proposal; the larger the project, the more people get looped into said decision. The process takes time. Weeks. Months.

You would need the entire novel completed plus a synopsis to sell to a traditional publisher. In non-fiction, you need a book proposal and sample chapters. It's doubtful that you can write a book, novel or play in one week; certainly not in five hours. A proposal and sample chapter deserve the better part of a month, maybe two, so that you can let the project sit then revise it with fresh eyes and insight. Those who self-publish need the time to gain perspective and revise in many drafts.

Contrast one week's time to small, easier-to-finish projects or queries. Writers embracing my approach have done their research, know a few editors in need of fillers, facts or fun stuff, and each week they submit an item to a different editor or market. The net effort soon reflects four or five chances toward acceptances that month, especially when you add more hours to the mix.

Which writer do you think has the likeliest chance toward a self-confident start and monetary validation? By virtue of favorable odds, the five-day, five-way writer has the fastest chance of acceptances in relation to attempts. This person can write numerous small items in the amount of time it takes others to produce the first draft of a longer submission, a novel chapter, or book proposal.

Stacking the odds in your favor isn't the only reason to start small. By consistently producing publishable material, you set yourself up to query editors regarding larger, better-paying assignments. You become a writer with a name, face, voice, and online/email presence. Editors will remember you when you pitch a feature in the months to follow.

Let's say you pitch to a different editor at the same publication. Editors talk. Your stating that you wrote for another staff editor may jump your query or material ahead of another writer unknown to the publication.

When you finish a longer-length project and sorely need a change of pace, writing filler assignments recharges your creative battery. Last but certainly not least with this approach, you develop pro-profit behavioral habits to produce, rather than procrastinate.

Fillers & Fun Stuff Defined

Take a look inside your favorite magazines, newsletters, or newspapers. Do you see those paragraph-size contributions? A humorous anecdote that evokes a smile or a surprise? How about household hints, recent studies, or seasonal tips, often set off with a large number, percentage or statistic destined to grab attention?

These overlooked gems are fillers and short bits. If these items are humorous, they qualify as laugh lines or as fun stuff. They don't drop out of nowhere. They see print because some writer— quite possibly you—understands an editor's need for quick takes on timely topics.

Fillers and short pieces make for fast sales, generating quicker payment. When you are published quickly your self-confidence soars because now an editor has recognized your potential.

Someone has said, "Hey, I like this," and has gone so far as to contact you, requisition a check, or issue a contract for one. The acquiring editor validated you financially and actually opened a door. Recognize the career value and future profit potential of both actions.

I doubt that you will deem fillers as a lucrative market. It's possible, but you still need your day job. Lucrative is as subjective a word here as profit was in a prior chapter.

A $25 sale means as much to the beginning writer as $2,500 does to a contributing editor of an upscale magazine. As I said in the beginning, this isn't about getting rich quickly. Money is subjective meaning something different for each writer.

Some short material pays $100 and beyond. Average magazine briefs span 200 to 500 words; sometimes, far fewer words, and the remuneration reflects the word count or space allotted. A dollar per word may put a smile on your face.

Secondary Payoffs & Paydays

Even though these paychecks will not put the bank on high alert, studying publications for filler material provides valuable opportunity for your creative mind. Hold onto that thought.

You will be able to tell, in many cases, whether brief material is staff-generated or freelance-driven. A byline often appears, preceded by an em dash (—writer's name). Check this byline against the publication masthead and list of staff writers. If the name does not appear as a staff member, there is a good chance the writer contributes as a freelancer. That writer could be you!

Brief material offers a fun, quick way to publish fact-filled tips, jokes, recipes, and inspirational stories. If that sounds too commercial and consumer-based when business writing is your primary interest, hold on...literally. Tips and inspirational stories appear in newsletters and trade publications. On hold messages comprise another means of brief matter that yields income; so too, might writing résumés or specific types of letters.

Worth mentioning one last time: your choosing to start small allows you entry to editors, a chance to establish and prove yourself with published clips. It also provides a way to re-focus your mind and still boost your bank account should you encounter creative blocks in longer, more intensive projects.

How to Generate Brief Matter

Short material puts brainstorming and writing to the clear-and-concise test. Much of what we read today is service-oriented journalism. It is material that makes the reader healthier, wealthier, wiser, more attractive, better liked, and well adjusted. Fillers and short projects are no different, providing that apprenticeship (and confidence boost) you will later need for tackling longer-length works.

Busy people often read fillers at a glance and put them to immediate use. Editors search for new spins on old topics. In addition, these subjects demand a reason to publish. So, if your filler is not timely or seasonal (such as August back-to-school tips) or service oriented (how the latest study applies to your health), then it must be newsworthy.

Keep an eye out for studies, research, and interesting angles. If not these three options, try a humorous approach. Decide also to put your heart on the page with a poignant memory or laugh a little if you commit an embarrassing moment to print (i.e., *your* mishap *not* someone else's mistakes).

Do realize that brief material competes with thousands of free news releases and public relations collateral material that invariably ends up on editor desks. What's going to cause an editor to acquire your information that will necessitate a check requisition instead of the free alternative?

Answer: a well-researched out-of-the-ordinary slant. When you see publications where you know staff writers have created brief matter, ask yourself how you might take the research that drew you in and slant it in a totally unique or local way. This I referred to as that other valuable opportunity.

I'll offer an example. While researching this book, *TIME* magazine ran a short item: "Barbies That Look More Like Real Girls." The news: a variety of ethnicities and body types now stocked toy shelves. The idea-hungry writer may think to write a filler or fun quiz; e.g., Which Barbie Are You Most Like? A holiday feature, a poll of parental feelings about the toy, or a collector's take on these dolls could also work.

If you want to delve deeper into the sociological or psychological impact, you could incorporate research about body image or query a women's magazine editor for a full-length feature. Right there, easily five possibilities toward profit.

Source Material

I tend to see news briefs or articles as wonderful source material. Find it in most any magazine or professional journal as well as in broadcast news reports. Quick, simple slices of Americana. USA Today Snapshots® has long been a repository of idea generation. Clip these out or take a picture with your phone when you spot one that germinates ideas. Always note the publication date.

Anniversaries of products or milestones also generate filler ideas. Years ago, I interviewed the late children's television host Fred Rogers for a Q&A article. I brainstormed many other angles and thought about which editors might feature this material. One immediate angle was Idlewild Park in Ligonier, Pennsylvania, home to a life-size Daniel Tiger's Neighborhood Exhibit to which kids ride the trolley and greet characters from the animated PBS program.

Trust me, there is and always has been much more to this fabulous family-oriented park, including picnic groves, theme areas, roller coasters and water slides. Many communities have amusement parks. However, this one had a perfect tie-in to the twenty-fifth anniversary of Mister Rogers' Neighborhood on public television. That became my news hook. People loved it. Many parenting publication editors sought ways to pay tribute when, sadly, Fred Rogers passed away. The theme park once again encouraged families to remember his legacy.

Writing Short Bits

Let the publication's suggested word count guide you. However, what a magazine editor considers short, a newsletter editor might consider long. I stated 50 to 500 words as average earlier in this chapter. Beyond 300 or 350 words, some editors view the submission as a mini-feature though I know some magazines whose columns come in at this length. Study publications. Follow writer's guidelines.

Each word must work hard. This takes practice, but once you develop the knack, you can crank these out more quickly. If your first draft runs long, put it aside for a few hours. This allows you to pinpoint a word here or a phrase there that can be cut without sacrificing meaning. Soon you will tighten the entire piece.

Journalism tenets have long included clarity and brevity. In order to achieve both, begin some sentences with active and imperative verbs, which help readers to focus upon and follow through with behavioral steps. Your readers will also appreciate the utility of such style. Thus, "to make cut-out cookies, mix the dough and roll it out." Next sentence: "Firmly press each cutter to create your desired shape." Longer, narrative prose deserves diverse sentence structure, so this style works best for brief how-to, stepped instruction.

Other ways to make your brief matter stand out include your incorporating percentages and numbers into your copy. Very often, the graphics people will enlarge this element on the page to draw in readers and grab their attention. Quote leading authorities, university studies, and bona fide news sources. A personal angle can also matter and stand out.

Woman's World, found at grocery checkouts, has published inspiration and encouragement as long as I can remember. In one recent issue, I spotted "Share your story: We'll pay $250 if we publish your feature story." Much of the time you can email these types of submissions. Pay ranges vary widely. Newsletters may offer $25 for a few sentences with quick, meaningful tips. *Reader's Digest* invites true stories submitted in 100 words or fewer. If editors choose your story, you'll be paid $100.

Writing Recipes

Kitchen hints or other valuable takeaways qualify as short bits and so do recipes. How do you test for an idea's originality? If you have heard it, then others have also. Exactly.

Test the hint on several friends of various ages and genders. Send product-related tips to manufacturers and send recipe ideas to companies whose ingredients are included. Just find out first whether the company pays for contributions before you share your nifty idea or delicious treat. If you're willing to submit material simply to obtain proof of being published, that's fine too.

One way to enter recipe writing may be to enter a contest or spot a call for contributions. What you learned earlier about useful, seasonal or fun angles also serves you here.

Create a recipe with a list of ingredients in the order they are needed and with a sequence in mind. There's nothing quite like frustrating a cook with hard-to-find, expensive ingredients; give commonly stocked alternatives when you can. With step-by-step instructions, you won't offend experienced cooks, but by leaving out necessary tips, you will annoy novices.

Vague measurements such as "a dash of nutmeg" remain too subjective. Stick with specific directions, with one possible exception being "salt and pepper to taste" because that's standard. Should you choose to add commentary or narrative to your recipe, do this at the very beginning, or preferably, at the end.

Contests that ask you for an essay (in addition to the recipe) are statistically easier to win because few entrants go to this effort. Your chances of winning might double. Food writers also share that if you change as few as three ingredients from another recipe, you have uniquely stamped your individual signature upon it. Now, it's deemed completely new.

Facts cannot be copyrighted. For recipe writers, this means that the ingredient list and the order in which they're listed and used cannot be either. Still, make it your own so that this is a new expression of a concept. Copyright does apply to other elements of a recipe or cookbook such as captions, explanations, comments, and methods. Obtain permission if you're reprinting and carefully cite each source.

Look to any culinary arts, women's, or parenting magazines, plus newspapers for recipe writing opportunities. Having said that, men's health magazines or those publications designed for budget-conscious families might also be a market you can pursue. Be creative. Just as you put a new spin on an old topic for fillers, do the same here.

Magazines for singles and senior citizens run single-serving recipes and tips on easy-to-prepare foods, the college crowd needs to master cooking with a Crock-Pot and microwave oven, and religious magazine readers might be adapting recipes to feed large congregations.

Meatless, fat-free, low-cholesterol, or gluten-free recipes are relevant for today's readers. If you can make something healthy and make it palatable for children, you've definitely scored big time for both parents and grandparents. Since we live in a gadget-filled world, brainstorm how to use the single-serving slow cooker, the waffle iron, crepe maker, frying machine, or ice cream maker for new, easy cooking and healthier desserts.

Food, cookware, and appliance companies feature recipes with products, and those Sunday coupon sections feature recipes that may or may not have been created in a corporate test kitchen.

Occasionally, greeting card companies feature recipes, especially during holidays. And if you're really blessed by two talents—creating written as well as culinary surprises—ask chefs, restaurants, caterers, nonprofit organizations, or even celebrities who might need help in compiling a cookbook.

Point out that by hiring a professional writer, the book will sell more copies, yielding higher profits for everyone involved. If no one of this caliber is available, undertake the role of editor with a community organization compiling a cookbook as a fund-raising project. It will be another credit to promote later. The marketing potential for recipe writing is fabulous as you're not confined to bookstores but can offer demonstrations in grocery or culinary stores as well.

With new dietary findings, and with our busy schedules, the demand for quick culinary magic is not likely to end. Just be sure to test any recipe before it leaves your office. Several times.

A simple slip such as using baking soda instead of baking powder could ruin a recipe. If you're skilled in photography and food styling, a tempting photograph might clinch the sale for you. In addition, keep up with the trends. Many people prefer to use fresh, organic, or gluten-free ingredients or recipes without refined sugar or flour.

Because the demand for new recipes and cookbooks has increased, so have the requirements. Cookbooks can no longer tempt readers with mere mouth-watering results. Readers often demand to know the calorie count, fat and sodium levels. Provide these, if at all possible.

Authors must craft entertaining descriptions, cultural information, tips for shopping and stocking a well-equipped (sometimes budget-conscious) kitchen. Assume your reader has no prior knowledge (or even fondness) for cooking, though sometimes, true foodies can constitute a magazine's market. That's a tougher audience for sure.

Of course, you must demonstrate knowledge, as nothing annoys a food editor more than a writer who doesn't know the first thing about cooking or the publication's reader.

Please Listen While Your Party Is Reached

We've all mumbled beneath our breath about the dreaded phone queue, listening to commercial messages and/or music while we wait for an attendant or information. Worse yet, the same music tracks over and over; the message we could recite in our sleep.

Yet when we gain valuable information, the wait time seems fortuitous rather than inconvenient. Even better, if we learn to create useful on-hold messages that serve the public, this garners deposits into our bank accounts. Keep reading this section for what it's like on the other side of that wait-time word fest.

Writers create these on-hold scripts for they understand the fine line between aggravation and information, quick turn-around for assistance, what makes a message "listenable," and how to incorporate multilingual scripts.

Rather than roll your eyes next time you hear, "We thank you for your patience, all operators are busy helping other customers," why not write something you deem less bothersome and indeed beneficial. These aren't high art, nor will they make you wealthy. They do serve as quick projects for writers wanting to sell their words, build credentials, and bring in some extra income. Convince a company or business owner the value of happy customers. This is key; the door may even open to more work.

As with all other writing avenues, I've outlined, do your homework. Record some of these and take notes. What do you like? What do you loathe? With any particular company what do YOU wish you knew? What's the original reason for your call and could the answer have been fodder for a new script. Surely if you have the question, others may also. Think about these elements, among all that follow. Commit to a brain escape of ideas and aim to make this a solid win for all concerned.

Writing Relevant On-Hold Scripts

On hold messages consist of far more than time filler. They combine customer service, draw attention to products or services, communicate with a customer base, and they become a part of a company's cohesive marketing strategy to increase sales.

Businesses that utilize on-hold messages are often seen as more customer-driven with the image-enhancement that this affords. Callers tend to stay on the line longer to initiate their intended purchase or request if they are offered something of value to listen to rather than mere music. Valuable content can mean hours the business is open or when calls can be accepted by a live operator, directions to the business, satellite locations, and of course, an online website and recent media.

Here, you can plant within the customer's mindset ideas like "our dedicated team," "we carry extensive selection," "get next day delivery," and of course, "we know your time is valuable and promise to be with you shortly." After all, there is a reason that business majors concentrating in marketing need to study psychology. Steve Jobs, the brilliant inventor, felt that people didn't really know what they wanted until you showed it to them. Here, you're telling them hopefully things (plural) that they will realize yes, they do need.

Some on-hold messages will alert the wait time until someone can handle the call or give an option to leave a message for a return call, at the customer's convenience. Occasionally these messages will contain snippets of company or corporate history, especially if the business celebrates a particular anniversary or achievement. It gives you a reason to tout those accomplishments, bragger's rights if you will.

Other means of varying the message may be to ask a "did you know" question or state a fact that will grab the listener's attention. If your client has a pest control business, for instance, you might wish to cite news reports about how a warmer than usual winter has spawned more mosquitoes or how spraying for deer ticks can prevent the spread of certain diseases, such as Lyme's Disease.

Most clients supply the basic information such as hours of operation and directions and then hire companies to craft their messages. We'll get to where you might sell your work in a moment, but for now, try your hand at a few sample scripts. They range from approximately 150 to 300 words but can be customized however the client desires. See if you like writing these. The time investment to try this is not as substantial as other types of assignments.

Increase your earnings by thinking creatively. Just as your best bets for fillers center around topical, seasonal, or new solution tips, the same applies to on-hold messages. Beyond "thank you for holding" and "your call is important to us," impart feel-good information about the company, feature trivia or product- or service-related hints and plant the thought of new purchases. The power of suggestion and outright directives pay off, e.g., consumers might forget that every six months they should change the batteries in their smoke detectors.

If you're writing an on-hold message for a hardware company, mention this as well as the need to stock up on extra Christmas lights in November or long after the holidays, lawn bags in the spring, and an extra propane tank this summer. Hint: Think ahead!

In this era of social media, on-hold messages point customers toward Facebook, Twitter, Instagram, Pinterest and other platforms where consumers can find answers easily from posted FAQs (frequently asked questions) and sometimes share in product/service enthusiasm. Direct customers to specific social media; ask them to engage by clicking on "contact the store," register for an event, or sign up for specials and discounts. Okay, this may seem like code for e-newsletter. Small business people, including authors, know the value of direct marketing this way.

If your content is very brief, try the three-prong format where your first sentence provides an introduction and includes the company name, sometimes location. It's followed by how something (product/service) will benefit people, and finally, calling the customers to action of some kind—to visit social media or a website, use a company's voice prompts, stay on the line for a representative's help, or take advantage of another means of assistance (phone message, email, fax).

Finding Clients

Where do you find potential clients? Using an online directory, type "on-hold messages" into the search box. When you hear messages, ask who supplies that company's on-hold tapes. Persistence will pay off when you finally discover the company's name, address, or telephone number. Pay ranges vary, but expect anywhere up to $100 per tape, possibly more if the work is more complex or must be updated frequently.

Seventy percent of all business calls are placed on hold for the average wait time of nearly one minute; ninety percent of callers hang up if offered mere silence. An on-hold message affords a tremendous marketing opportunity for products or services.

Put your best audio-writing skills to the test. Writing for brevity helps because every word must work, each being the lowest common denominator—that is, skip the fifteen-letter word for the five-letter word that is easier to pronounce and comprehend quickly. Always read your copy aloud. You should time out your scripts with a stop watch because each will be read and recorded. Assign male and female roles, if necessary, and supply the pronunciation just as you would in writing broadcast copy. You don't want the producers and voice talent to complain about your difficult script.

These scripts span anywhere from a three-minute tape featuring six or eight messages to a six-minute version using between ten and twelve messages. With holidays, seasonal sales, related trivia, company-offered tips, and other events, no doubt there is the chance for constant updating if the client likes your work. Most writers email or fax drafts to clients and await revisions. With approved changes, plans to record the messages come next. Clients receive new on-hold tapes according to their contracts, but the terms could be monthly, bimonthly, quarterly, or as needed (if some special circumstance develops).

Writers who succeed at this venue say that volume and speed are integral to earning more substantial payment. If they can craft a six-minute script in half an hour, they could be making between $30 and $80 an hour or beyond.

Résumé Writing

Earlier in this book, I mentioned how job changers and virtually any employee who wants to rise in a career needs a good résumé to capsulize experience, education, interests, and effort.

If you have a day-job such as school or college counselor, human resource staff member or teacher/mentor, your credentials may help attract clients. However, generalist writers can add résumé writing to their business cards.

After I earned my college degree, I faced a recessionary economy and so did workers who had spent years in industries such as steel, in my hometown of Pittsburgh. While I looked for other employment myself, I advertised at a community college, where there was both a career center and a small business development center. I guess you could say that since I didn't readily find a job, I created at least one more side gig.

I helped several job seekers take years of odd jobs and employment transitions, that they were forced into merely to make ends meet and sent them away with a document they could use to better present themselves, lessening time gaps. Above all, I listened to them carefully, took notes, and asked questions.

A good résumé writer will also have a keen eye for what the job seeker shows on paper. Most clients have some rudimentary document that might provide you for a first pass at this project. Look to improve parallel construction, phrases that could be made stronger with action verbs, gaps that could be filled, and volunteer work that could be highlighted.

Advise clients against cutesy email and help them to limit bullet points per item to five, no more than six if possible.

Quantify results with numbers and percentages whenever possible as numbers and money shouts out that the candidate is qualified. For those uncomfortable departures, the savvy writer will offer phrases such as "will explain personally" or "prefer to keep confidential until interview."

Gear the résumé to the company culture and write that your client spearheaded projects, showed initiative, was involved with team building and leadership. Describe stellar communication, both written and verbal, as well as problem-solving skills. As I describe shortly, these are often important keywords to include.

In *1,001 Phrases You Need to Get A Job,* Nancy Schuman and Burton Jay Nadler provide useful guidance, keywords, and what they call influencing phrases. These authors have done much of the brainstorming for you and your clients, going a step before and after with cover letter and interviewing suggestions. I especially liked the words targeted to specific industries and their giving the green light to certain expressions.

Many times, job seekers must apply online. This means you need to create a résumé that will upload well without extraneous characters. Scan what you generated into a PDF. This will keep your formatting the way you created it. You might also provide one version for a print shop and one for online uploading.

MONEY featured expert résumé tips in March 2018 driving home the fact that large companies vet their job-seeking candidates through applicant tracking systems (ATS). Once uploaded, résumés get scanned by an ATS for keywords that apply to the particular job. Since the software scans vertically, center as much data as possible.

Many candidates may be taken out of consideration before a human company representative can read the document. Therefore, it makes sense to tailor various résumés should your client have many career options. Good for the writer's revenue, for sure.

Word processing programs offer templates but it's a good idea to have résumé writing books for all kinds of circumstances and careers, those just graduating from training programs, college and graduate school, those returning to work after time off, or when your client transitions into another line of employment.

You want to have examples at the ready when you must explain job gaps, combine a series of smaller or much earlier jobs, and make volunteer, even homemaking duties, appear as relevant and business-acceptable as possible.

When a client seeks work in creative fields, such as graphic design, fashion, and the arts, ratchet up your own creative ideas since companies will look for this element.

Design your own unique templates to reuse with different types of clients and to show choices when you first meet people. A portfolio of many types of résumés will pay for itself in helping you to win over more clients.

Five

Sentimental Payday

People will forget what you said, people will forget what you did, but people will never forget how you made them feel.
— Maya Angelou, poet

According to the Greeting Card Association (GCA) in Washington, D.C., annual retail sales in the United States total between seven to eight billion dollars. Yes, billion.

The *Atlanta-Journal Constitution* reported in December 2016 that 1.6 billion cards were sold in retail stores for the Christmas holidays, making it the largest card-selling holiday trailed by Valentine's Day.

Before moving too far into this market, here is my rule. The first one or two companies you think of should perhaps be your last, at least in terms of submissions. Indeed Hallmark, purveyor of cards, gifts, even made-for TV movies, is a company based in Kansas City, Missouri. Hallmark along with American Greetings make up eighty-two percent of the U.S. greeting card market.

That's not to say that knowledge of these companies and their standards won't help you, but I have seen far too many writers become discouraged because they set their sights on an industry giant. Hallmark, for instance, has a substantial and talented cadre of staff writers. Those who leave the company, let's say to raise families or semi-retire, sometimes end up as one of the few freelancers who garner assignments.

The average writer's best chances to sell card ideas and get published lies with smaller companies, many of whom feature edgy, risqué, or sentimental verses. Some may even buy design concepts. Realize that the catchy phrase you conjured for a card may land with an editor who needs napkin or mug slogans instead. The results of your pithy captions may amaze you.

If you're a poet, you won't be surprised that poetry isn't easy to publish for payment. Poems might find a home in collections produced by small presses, literary journals, or books of poetry. Some of these might not generate a paycheck. If payment is your primary objective, shift your mindset into the greeting card industry, particularly to companies that align with your values.

This brings me to my second important caveat. Greeting card editors do not really consider their editorial product to be poetry, which traditionally is a writer's unique self-expression. Greeting cards, on the other hand, express the sentiments of thousands through the creator. You, as writer, act as a conduit.

Greeting Your Way to Income

As I write this section, Avanti Press, Blue Mountain Arts, Calypso Cards, DaySpring, Oatmeal Studios, Paper Bandit Press, Smart Alex, Up with Paper, and Viabella seem to be viable in terms of freelance contributions.

I also suggest regional paper product companies such as Cape Shore, Inklings, Paperie, Rifle Paper Co. that produce theme merchandise. You might find some shop along the Atlantic seaboard that carries nautical, sea-themed cards, napkins, and products. One based in mountain states might have an entirely different need. Turn the product over to discover a market.

Know the inventory, study the writer's guidelines, and have a clear understanding of how the editor prefers to receive your submissions. Submitting via email has changed what at some companies used to be the standard 3x5 index card submission.

Going back two centuries, Louis Prang, "father of American Christmas cards," became the first to mass-produce greeting cards. The Greeting Card Association (www.greetingcard.org) hosts The Louie Award, the card equivalent to an Oscar, each May. Different categories are judged on imagination, emotional impact, artistry, ability to sell, and the harmony struck between the card's visual elements and verse. Top-winning cards have been featured on network morning shows.

No matter how fast paced our society is, people's emotions remain the driving force behind motivations and actions. Greeting cards offer the antidote for a sagging spirit. If you can think of your work as a real emotional boost when people need it most, you're doing much more than adding income and accomplishment to your career. While it's true that electronic cards and Facebook posts step in and suffice as birthday greetings, actual products have not completely gone out of vogue.

Greeting card writing truly qualifies as a faster cash prospect. Top companies pay the most ($100 to $200 per verse), but of course, your competition is much steeper there. Hundreds of companies pay $10 to $100 for a conventional or traditional verse. If you're selling humor or longer material, you can usually count on a bigger check of perhaps $40 to $300.

Understanding the Business Side

Writers who hear these rates are typically thrilled. They understand that the industry pays no royalties. Unless you're so successful that you license popular material, it's standard to sell all rights. But we're talking about a sentence or two. In most cases, that is the typical length.

You may bristle at giving up rights; but imagine the company if it didn't operate this way. It would pay for a verse and spend a lot of money to emblazon it onto cards, T-shirts, or calendars. Then writers could turn around and sell it to another vendor to put on similar merchandise. Not a good way to conduct business.

If your material is lengthy and you balk at selling all rights, consider your idea's potential as a mini-book with a traditional publisher or through reputable self-publishing platforms.

Before accepting material, a greeting card editor will send you a disclosure form where you state that what you submit is original. Sign and return it promptly. After you sell specific verses, more paperwork follows for that specific caption.

Visit different gift shops, bookstores, grocers, pharmacies, and party supply stores to research card companies and verses. Internet research helps, but nothing replaces being able to physically read the card and turn it over since the backside often contains useful information for writers. Look at the range of verses and the various lines of products. Don't limit your search. Mail-order companies specialize in cards, posters, mugs, T-shirts, note pads, and beverage napkins. Seek out the serious, the silly, the sexy, the religious, and everything in between.

Greeting card companies publish writer's guidelines and needs lists, especially once you begin working with particular editors. Request guidelines by writing to each company with a self-addressed, stamped envelope, otherwise known as an SASE or, more efficiently, look on the Internet.

The Greeting Card Association in the United Kingdom (www.greetingcardassociation.org.uk) suggests that you fit as many captions as possible on one sheet of paper and number them each.

Do not send more than six samples in an A4 envelope (4x6). In the U.S., a #10 business envelope is traditionally the standard size. Each page should contain your name and address, and all content should appear typewritten in a simple, plain font. Accompany all submissions by an SASE (you'll want to receive the rejected captions for your records). A cover letter briefly introduces you, but it doesn't need to say much more.

Again, check each company's guidelines to determine if you need to use 3x5 cards, single typed pages, or digital submissions. In February 2016, *Business Insider* interviewed Diana Manning, a greeting card writer for Hallmark. She reported that the process has gone digital, away from the physical captions typed out and sent through the postal service.

Caption Construction

All captions begin as ideas. Keep a journal as these gems pop into your mind. Later, you'll concentrate upon word association and brainstorming. One helpful exercise: take a blank sheet of paper and divide it into several columns. From left to right along the top, write different occasions for sending cards such as new baby, wedding, and woman-to-woman friendship along your paper. Under each occasion, list as many words as you can associate with each category. Capture all thoughts, dismissing none in this free-associating process.

Set your goal to obtain a range of emotions, words, and phrases that you will have at your disposal. Try putting a new spin on an old problem just as you may have done when writing brief non-fiction material. Yet a third approach: look at a subject from the opposite perspective. Regardless of your technique, you must convey a greeting. No greeting, no sale.

Draw upon your own circumstances and gain sensitivity to create powerful messages. Take yourself back to the innocent child bursting with the holiday thoughts. Think of the songs that resonate with you. What is it about these lyrics that moves you?

If you've gone through difficult life passages, such as divorce, caretaking, grieving the death of a loved one, or loss of a job, try to unearth those raw emotions. What helped you through? Life's sorrows can increase our capacity for compassion.

Perhaps the single-most important aspect of a sellable caption is the me-to-you message—the feeling people have that the sentiment was written just for them. Remember the "who cares?" I asked that in the journalism chapter as I encouraged writers to have a substantial audience. Without enough recipients who can relate to your sentiment, in that me-to-you way, your caption will not sell commercially.

A me-to-you message can be funny, but never so sarcastic as to be perceived as a dig. Mean intent, political, ethnic, or other insensitivity will get you nowhere. Write to build up, not tear down. If you're uncertain how a particular caption will be taken, test your humor on a variety of others. Stuck creating me-to-you messages? Write down what you're trying to convey without the right words, rhyme, or meter. Work with it until it flows.

We will discuss crafting gags in the next chapter, but the power of three applies also when creating captions. The human brain seems to best accept information broken down into three parts. For example, for a business startup/congratulations card, you could write, "Three little words every businessperson loves to hear . . . It's tax deductible!" The first phrase here would be intended for the outside of the card; the last three words for the inside verse, followed by congratulations on your new venture or some other clever greeting.

With humor, divide verses for the proper comedic effect, enough to deliver a laugh or a groan without giving away the punch line of the outside verse or first-second parts. What if you don't have three levels of inspiration? Keep at this until perhaps you do. If you can draw upon an example from real life, try stretching it to fit the format.

Other Skills

Two additional ways to communicate a message include drawing comparisons and reworking a phrase or a cliché. Riddles and rhymes, if you're skilled at using these techniques, offer even more caption construction options.

Rhyme and meter can enhance a me-to-you message, or it can get in the way. If you can make it move, that is great, but don't force the meter. Allow the accent to fall on the syllable where it would naturally fall in everyday speech.

Manning, in her *Business Insider* interview, shared that she got her Hallmark spot after four days of interviews and learned later that it was her rhyme and meter skills plus a sense of structure that got her the nod and the job.

Bible verses often inspire you to craft religious captions. If your verse reflects a specific Biblical passage, be sure to cite the chapter and verse as well as the translation you used.

Deepen the connection between the card sender and recipient. Take a verse you've crafted. Be direct. Specific. You might start with a fact, such as "It's your birthday . . ." and build the sentiment around that. Use a problem such as mixed feelings about growing older as your starting point on the outside. Then follow with something completely new, fresh sarcasm or another sentiment inside.

Finally, try alliteration ("She sells seashells by the seashore"), literary inspiration (taking a great first sentence and expanding with a verse that is fresh and new), or surprise (romantic promise on the outside, something silly inside).

Verse Variants

Most cards have both an outside and inside verse, though some have only one. An "O:" stands for the outside verse and what follows, and an "I:" stands for inside verse and its contents.

Sandwiched between your code and your outside verse might be a graphic idea as depicted in an illustration, possibly a photograph. Mind you, editors aren't obligated to use your graphic idea, but if you feel your art concept could sell the verse, include it. Your editor may see the sentiment's use, however, for an entirely different self-expression product.

Beginner mistakes: Ignorance of industry, for starters. Point-of-purchase stores and catalog or online companies have different sales goals and caption needs.

Your local card rack probably features a general anniversary card, as well as happy first anniversary, celebrating a silver one, and happy fiftieth cards. That is four different kinds of anniversary categories for a retail-driven card company. But your catalog- or Internet-based retailer may only feature a general, one-size-fits-all anniversary product. A "thank-you-to-the-teacher" card is too specific for a general product line. Save specific ideas for particular professionals or niche occasions for point-of-purchase companies.

Another mistake: allowing one editor's negative response to squash your creativity. With any rejection, it helps to know why you were rejected, and if the editor scrawls on her reply that the company already had similar material, you know it wasn't you or your efforts. This isn't something worth grieving over. Send it to other companies. Heed any advice you're given. Perhaps by changing only a word or two, you can make this a quicker sale next time you submit it. Never underestimate the power of the rewrite, if that is what it takes to make your work shine.

Practice patience. Some editors will return a set of rejected captions, yet hold others, routing them to colleagues for their feedback. In fact, many beginners fail to realize that decisions get made collectively, that is, with other editorial team members. Your job is to turn one editor on to your caption. That editor, in turn, takes it to a meeting or circulates it within the department.

While editors make their decisions, which could take months, unfortunately, keep your creative energy alive. Send off another batch of captions to another company. But don't submit the same captions to multiple companies simultaneously because this is a surefire way to alienate all editors who may end up wanting to purchase the same verse. No writer needs that headache.

While greeting card writers are not required to submit art, the more visual you think, the more money you make. Small companies may like both skills, but major ones already have a working stable of illustrators and photographers.

Ponder the following summary of tips as a brief review:

- Spot trends and keep current. Scour magazine advertisements, product catalogs, and even the newspapers to get a pulse on what is hot and what is not.
- Extend your skills to long, heartfelt and short quips.
- Consider additional avenues for poetry. Captions might be a different way of thinking initially, but you may find that editors could use your talents.
- Visit card company websites to view their guidelines and familiarize yourself with the sample captions. Do the same research in person, at racks of cards. Trust me, you will never look at in-store displays the same way again.
- Keep an idea journal. Cultivate the talent of thinking visually so that there is enough imagery for your editor, an illustrator, or a photographer to do the rest.
- Recycle rejected captions. If they continue to meet rejection, analyze them. Perhaps they lack universal appeal or a me-to-you message. Might you repackage these for successful sale elsewhere?
- Don't forget self-expression products as a way of making more money with your captions. Short one-liners will do.
- Develop a thick skin. Even veteran greeting card writers report that at least fifty to sixty percent of their verses do not ever get printed; but of course, the others can and do.
- Realize that this is a work-for-hire industry. You will relinquish all rights to your verses, unless otherwise stated. Insisting on anything else brands you as a newbie.

Professional Letter Writing or Email Services

If you are good at generating caring sentiments, correspondence writing is a natural extension of for your talents and bank account.

Who doesn't have time to write a note himself? You would be surprised. Well-written letters or appeals to key decision makers can clinch a desired outcome.

Those writers who advertise their letter writing services are sometimes called upon to draft job application letters, college essays, admission paperwork to coveted clubs or contests. The phrasing book recommended in the last chapter (and in the resource section) may prove quite handy.

Don't forget about complaint letters when major products or services have not lived up to expectation or to elected officials when a lot might be riding on that member's advocacy and vote.

Around the holidays, you might write the family's annual newsletter or ghostwrite a family history for a special anniversary or reunion.

In fact, some letter writers have been called upon to pen love letters and then the ultimate one, these days spoken before an audience and even videotaped: the marriage proposal.

Think Cyrano de Bergerac, hiding his identity yet openly revealing emotion. Imagine, your passionate words read many times over, pulled from a folded stack in a wooden box of loving memories or shown years later to the couple's children. Ghostwriters often assist a couple to create personal wedding vows or creative birth announcements when the family expands.

On the flip side, some writers offer their services for those dreaded tasks such as drafting the Dear Jane or Dear John letter. They might gain work to tackle other tough topics such as encouragement to be sent to a friend or colleague battling illness or a sympathy note after the untimely or even anticipated death of loved ones.

The families of the deceased, overwhelmed by grief, life changes, sudden shock and settling estates, may welcome a compassionate and articulate writer willing to thank those who reached out with kind gestures or gifts during their time of need.

At first glance, one might not ordinarily think that professional letter writing would ever find its way onto a business card or LinkedIn profile, but hopefully with the examples I've cited, you will see that plenty of writers do profit from such work.

Sometimes when even the most educated, high-ranking, and successful executives sit down to commit pen to paper, their minds draw a blank. If they can afford to hire this task out and enough is riding on the outcome, they would much rather you write material for them.

Writers who enjoy the romantic classics of centuries past often revel in the genteel declarations of love and admiration. They are often fans of *Pride and Prejudice, Gone with the Wind* and Shakespeare's *Much Ado about Nothing.* Before you go this way with your phrasing, however, talk to the guy who is proposing. Possibly talk to one of the woman's best friends to find out preferences as well.

Ask for advice, what would be welcomed, what not. Find out if humor is okay and how much. Review how the couple met, what attracted them to one another, and what makes each of them so special at first meeting and at present.

Lastly, be original, plan, and help the recipient who will be delivering your well-crafted proposal to rehearse the words until they become second nature. Of course, you add this time into your fee, but let's face it. You can't control the delivery, but you want it to be memorable, for the couple's sake…and yours.

The Business Side of Correspondence

To be successful at this, tap into how clients uniquely express themselves. Ask for samples of prior correspondence, email communication, and take notes while talking with them by telephone or in person.

Confidentiality, of course, is paramount. You will become privy to private matters, family secrets and tragedies, maybe even scandalous laundry. Trust becomes vital, and it will be a prime selling point when marketing the need for and the benefits of your services.

One drawback of selling your best wit or using your most heartfelt sentiments on those you may never meet is that your own social media or communication may suffer as a result. Maybe; maybe not.

Clearly, this kind of work is best suited for those with plenty of words to both share and spare. And of course, the client may reuse your phrasing. Nothing much you can do about that. Do a great job and repeat business or referrals to others may come your way.

Browsing the website Upwork.com, I spotted a post that sought an experienced email copywriter to produce effective templates for a high-tech company. These email scripts would be used to solicit new clients and engage dormant ones. The company requested a portfolio and examples of the copywriter's best work.

For the cost of a calligraphy class, you may be able to charge slightly higher considering the content and added visual appeal your work would offer to your finished product.

In this era of social media, the best marketing sites for you to attract work include LinkedIn, Elance, Twitter, and Facebook, among others. For those crafting marriage proposals, word-of-mouth will get this moving, but social media and video evidence may be one of your best marketing tools.

At conferences and in author promotion tips, I see increasing evidence of how video endorsements gain traction on social media and websites. Those posts attract the most views, likes, and shares, which extends organic reach.

Shore Thing Publishing
PROOF COPY

Six

Money Is a Joke

*Everything is funny, as long as it's
happening to somebody else.*
— Will Rogers, humorist

W hat famous laugh lines still put a smile on your face?
Maybe they are from movies, books, your own friends
or family with hilarious memories that get retold time
and again. Before I move on, let's see if you can place these
famous lines with their origin:

"I've a feeling we're not in Kansas anymore."

"I will not exploit, for partisan political purpose, my
opponent's youth and inexperience."

"Frankly, my dear, I don't give a damn."

"You're a sad, strange little man, and you have my pity."

"I'll have what she's having."

"Just keep swimming."

Six examples surely make my point. These lines found their
way into pop culture and resurface long after—catch the answers
—*The Wizard of Oz,* Ronald Reagan, *Gone with the Wind,* Buzz
Lightyear, *When Harry Met Sally,* and *Finding Nemo* made them
all quite memorable.

Even when famous lines were never uttered to reap laughter,
we now use them in situations to lighten tension. The authors of
these never factored in the power of stellar lines. If they only
knew how archived everywhere their creations have become.

We can piggyback on these efforts if we take well-known phrasing and add our own punch lines to them. Indeed, editors like to infuse a bit of wit or whimsy into their pages. They appreciate the humorous anecdote, the one-liner, an exaggeration, a bit of well-placed sarcasm, or something so understated that it literally stands out. Nowhere is wit more important than an ending that is supposed to reap a laugh.

Humor Markets

Reader's Digest is perhaps the best-known home for jokes, gags and funny quotes, and the publication pays $25 per item published in the magazine.

For any truly funny story, the pay rate rockets to $100. Just as the two most popular greeting card companies may be long shots, this well-known publication receives such a sheer volume of submissions that you must consider how and where you wish to spend your limited time. Go after smaller ones, too.

Magazines are not your only market for carefully crafted punch lines. You might sell your work to politicians, public speakers, speechwriters, radio disc jockeys, cartoonists or other publishers. In serious projects, humor often lends itself to the perfect lead or closing that can grab a reader or leave a favorable and lasting impression.

This section shows you how and offers some caution. With the mission to make money, you must guard against putting a funny remark out there cavalierly. Once posted, it could be lifted. Use joke banks or Internet forums with a great deal of restraint.

Study the Craft

To research what elicits laughs and what begets groans or silence, visit local comedy clubs and watch comedians on television. The same applies to radio and to the morning hosts of radio drive times, the most popular listening hours.

Read and learn from interviews with comedians and their memoirs. Watch the morning and evening news. Trivia is grist for the humor mill, as evidenced by metropolitan newspapers that publish a New Year's list of what's in and what's out. Let pop culture and trends guide you, even presidential elections. That's taking a cue from *Saturday Night Live (SNL)*.

When the first President Bush left office, the game of horseshoes was replaced by American fascination with the saxophone (a Clinton pastime). Becoming our 44th president, Barack Obama relieved job pressures through pickup basketball whereas Bush 43 rode a mountain bike. Laura Bush advocated for education and worked on literacy whereas Michelle Obama brought gardening, healthy eating and staying fit into focus.

Such minutiae can tell you what's trending or re-tweeted. How many times a post gets shared on Facebook can tell you what's caught people's eye. It may prove popular, but of course, not convey accuracy. We do know that scandal, traumatic or embarrassing incidents tend to trend well, but making light of such matters may display garishness and prove to be detrimental to innocent others and to yourself if the incident you use is false.

"Use sarcasm sparingly, with good taste, and never to hurt," I wrote in *Overcoming Passive-Aggression* because such comments are only funny when understood by all within a supportive relationship or perhaps in standup comedy.

Let your best judgment discern the difference between fun and poor taste. Be sure readers understand "hey, I'm kidding" when you write something that people could react strongly to.

Understatement serves a purpose to write something comedic when the tenor or talk of the day remains serious. Let's say a big storm blew through. Using understatement, you could write, "We got a little rain recently, didn't we?" Commenting upon a neighborhood that's visibly run down, you might say, "Looks as if there's a lot of opportunity around here."

Courting the Chuckle

What exactly qualifies as funny? Almost anything, but one of the surest bets in any successful joke remains poking fun at yourself or sheer parody. Shared human experience often bonds people together no matter how diverse their backgrounds. It's as if making a confession of your own foibles invites readers (or listeners) to laugh along with you. But beware.

We dislike it when others glorify offensive material or mock others insensitively. While we might laugh at a skit on Comedy Central or *Saturday Night Live,* that same material might seem cruel if presented (and cemented) in print.

The confession of idiosyncrasies works well to introduce a topic that might otherwise come across as a complaint. Exaggeration or hyperbole (extreme exaggeration) also spawns humor and makes a point. It's not very funny when your two-year-old or teenager whines, yet in comedy, if you imitated some powerful figure whining, it might. Pointing out the outrageous things, which are violations to everyday benign existence, can summon a chuckle (often Jerry Seinfeld's comedic formula).

An ordinary story retold becomes more fun if you add hyperbole such as "I had fifty million phone calls this afternoon" or "the guy's leather shoes looked as if they came from the dinosaurs themselves."

You might have the world laughing with you if you compare your stock earnings in a poor economy to a third world country that most see as the bastion of evil, but it's too risky if it comes across as culturally insensitive. Thus, knowing the pulse, the tenor of your audience counts. Humor is often nothing more than drama, just exaggerated.

Stumped for ideas? Look to children's behavior, home repairs, politics, headline moments, foibles of the rich and famous, even aging and sex as fodder for your next gag. Or make it a combination. Exaggerate your own misfortunes, quirks, biases, or shortcomings. Have an opinion. Focus upon social or cultural inequality—real or imagined—because this is often on people's minds. Comedians can get away with expressing these.

We tend to laugh at the union of two incongruous things, e.g., "nervous like a pregnant nun." That's because the two thoughts don't juxtaposition well. Often, funny phrases work because of their unpredictability. You've presented one part that the reader/listener expects, and when you surprise them with incongruity, you elicit a laugh.

The comedy writing style should err to the concise. The longer you set up the joke, the more the audience expects, and greater risk you create if it's not as funny as you presume. Build to the end. Your punch line is everything and the reason for each item preceding it. Make sure you have a powerful punch line before you even start writing. Without it, your joke will surely flop.

Melvin Helitzer has co-authored *Comedy Writing Secrets.* He has a handy mnemonic device of THREES. This formula stands for: target, hostility, realism, exaggeration, emotion, and surprise.

Essentially, comedy targets something specific or challenges the status quo. Many appreciate humor as an antidote to hostility. It very much is just that. It's also real, quite frank, and very often, a statement of the bitter truth.

When we exaggerate, we stretch our imagination. It's usually comical. As we'll discuss next, there's a tension that builds in the comedic formula and it touches people's emotion in the process.

Finally, comedy contains the element of surprise. Gene Perret, who wrote *The New Comedy Writing Step by Step* and numerous other books, has likened comedy to mentally pulling the rug out from under each person in the audience. Indeed, there is a startle reaction we hope to gain when we lob or hear a joke.

Overall, stick with those topics you handle best. If creating something off-color is too far a stretch for you, then stick to what you're most comfortable poking fun at and surfacing.

Magic Effect of Three

A sense of rhythm is paramount to good humor writing as discussed with greeting cards where timing works in sets of three. Our brains absorb information best this way. In fact, when offered a list of four or five data points, most people become overwhelmed with information overload.

To build tension that a good punch line depends upon, add a second onto the first, and stop with a third example. Author William Lang developed a comedic theory with three elements better known as SAP, short for setup (prep stage), anticipation (where you use triple examples) and punch line (the payoff).

Helitzer was quoted in the *Austin Business Journal* about what he called triples—three alternative solutions consecutively as magic. He recommended no less, no more than three to sustain what he dubbed "the roll." This rule of three applies to characters in an anecdote. The line "There was a priest, a minister, and a rabbi…" comes to mind. Four people in there would slow down the natural cadence or that roll. So, three is the writer's lucky number based on brain processing as well as pleasing rhythm.

The concept isn't exclusive to comedy. It's been used in serious works. Thomas Jefferson identified life, liberty, and the pursuit of happiness while Martin Luther King Jr. repeated his famous refrain three times: "Free at last! Free at last! Thank God Almighty, we're free at last!"

Since comedy is the topic in this chapter, I'll close this section with an example from Ellen DeGeneres, who once said, "My grandmother started walking five miles a day when she was 60. She's 97 now and we don't know where the hell she is."

Your words need to please readers well enough to create a sale—three examples, three anecdotes, three comparisons or exaggerations. Fit this concept into your comic perspective.

Can Comedy Pay?

Steve Calechman, a journalist, reached out to me for an interview regarding my passive-aggression book. Finding his website, I spotted the work he had done in comedy. After he interviewed me, I asked Steve about comedy and he sent me his insights.

"I've been a journalist and standup comedian both for about 25 years," Steve said. "The writing pays most of the bills. I started out freelancing for a community newspaper and got hired as a reporter in the mid-1990s, and then went to a startup magazine. Six months later, I was let go. I've been a freelancer ever since, writing for magazines (both print and online). I've worked for universities, written content for companies, and taught an adult education standup class for years."

"With comedy, I write and perform my own stuff," he continued. "I've worked in any place that has a microphone and even some that didn't, meaning clubs, bars, theaters, temples, and even once upon a ladder in a zoo."

Calechman wrote for sports teams, where he admits that payment was tickets he gladly accepted. The New England Patriots used him as a correspondent for an online show, a gig that found him interviewing the press, doing segments in the parking lot, on the field, and in the stadium with fans as well.

Standup comedy introduced him into the acting world with commercials and a bit part in the beginning of *The Proposal*. It was just long enough to be asked "was that you?" he joked.

Learn from the Masters

Commuting to work, I've listened to my share of audio books. I loved Tina Fey reading *Bossypants,* where a Midwest girl's naiveté endeared readers. Fey presents many teenage rites of passages as a laugh track we could appreciate well before her tour of duty on Weekend Update or as Sarah Palin seeing Alaska from her house on SNL.

There are memoirs written by those who started small, penning others' comedy, like Fey's career began. These books teach about comedic style in between autobiographical passages. Dave Barry is extensively published and surely you will learn his style from books and archived articles. Ellen DeGeneres has written books but also has video archives to watch from her television appearances.

Steve Martin, who started his career with magic and stand-up comedy, moved into movies and became a pop culture fixture for decades. *Born Standing Up: A Comic's Life* recounts how this wasn't always so, how he plodded on from Disneyland to the Bird Cage Theatre at Knott's Berry Farm, and how Johnny Carson's program and *Saturday Night Live* presented career-changing opportunities. And yet, these turns of fate took time to effect Steve's stardom.

In addition to his comedy writing books, Gene Perret has written numerous compilations of one-liners for toastmasters and public speakers. Comedy USA features interviews by standup comics and others involved in the comedy industry. It also lists published resources to guide you further.

Where to Sell Laugh Lines

Local and national comics continually search for fresh, original humor to keep their gigs alive. Since the national, somewhat more famous set, don't have a lot of time to write their own material, they often turn to freelance joke writers.

Public speakers and politicians need these laugh lines just as much. Most metropolitan areas have comedy clubs where the entertainers might need a creative boost. Radio personalities also rely upon freelance material to make their morning shows, especially, wake us up.

Type "comedy network" or "radio network" into an Internet search engine to find outlets. The National Association of Comedians, LLC is designed for stand-up comedians, improvisational groups and comedic actors. The professional association provides group discounts on health insurance and helps members attain knowledge through education, other career boosts, as well as networking.

In comedy writing, you'll often be paid by the joke or monologue. It's not uncommon for buyers to purchase a few jokes and pass on the rest. If that happens, increase your sales by contributing the rejected jokes to a gag sheet, frequently used by radio personalities. While this doesn't pay much, you'll recoup something for your creative effort.

Most laugh lines, jokes, or silly anecdotes are submitted in batches, up to approximately a dozen in each batch. Send each on a separate sheet with your name, address, telephone number, and e-mail on each submission. If your editor prefers electronic submissions, follow that preference.

Parody Entertainment

We've all had that moment when a certain song or lyric won't escape our minds. If you enjoy satire plus music—chorus, verses, lyrics—one market to consider is parody song writing, composing, and/or performing. Song projects showcase well a writer's creativity and lyrical skills. They're often done for the purpose of humor or education, particularly when a teacher wishes to help students connect to and retain information in a fun, new way.

Late night comic Jimmy Fallon has brought song parody into his repertoire, often using what news headlines provide. He impersonated Bruce Springsteen with a parody of "Born to Run," which dealt with the New Jersey traffic scandal dubbed Bridgegate on one of his shows.

ZDoggMD is a former emergency room physician who has successfully parodied various pop-culture phenomena such as Harry Potter and TED Talks. Medical personnel have long used a form of gallows humor to get through the heavy, intense nature of their jobs. While the ZDoggMD audience clearly understood the dangers about Ebola, they could laugh when he sung about it to the Kinks' "Lola." Artists might weave some truth and fact into parodies. After searching online at YouTube, you can peruse several more Fallon and ZDoggMD examples.

I've known people who took personal, funny information that others provided, wrote a parody and then coupled it with well-known musical tunes. The more detail regarding the recipient of the intended song, the more developed the finished product turned out. These original parody gifts can be sung at milestone events such as big birthdays, anniversaries or retirements, particularly if you have the singing talent to carry that off. It can be a part of one's freelance business or a separate side gig.

Crafting A Parody

Nothing replaces listening to other good parody songs if you wish to begin writing these yourself. This way, you can decide if humorous or fact-driven, informational parodies are your style.

Remember once again the "who cares" question posed earlier. You must have an intended audience albeit it doesn't have to be large. The type of audience will guide you.

To craft an effective parody:

Select a tune that's recognizable. Some writers choose older tunes that may be in the public domain by now; others go for current pop hits. Regardless, pick something you like. A song with distinctly separate verses and choruses may prove easier to parody. Should you decide to make them funnier, some of the comedy advice presented in that section may help. Brainstorming and word association are fairly straightforward.

Leave some phrases or lyrics unchanged. Especially if your new redesign takes advantage of a double-entendre or a double meaning, keep the original. Otherwise, capitalize on the rhyming nature of your material (and obviously the rhythms), make up your own story, or add facts in an amusing summary (the Jimmy Fallon example did a few of these things).

Work from beginning to the end to assure that your song makes complete sense. This advice applies when you labor over verses yourself. Musicians can record or make tracks themselves. This grants more creative control over the finished product, but it might not be for you.

Do sufficient research regarding copyright and fair use. Stanford University Library has a concise overview of fair use, explaining the "copying of copyrighted material done for a limited and transformative purpose, such as to comment upon, criticize, or parody a copyrighted work."

Investigate other issues. This includes your producing a derivative work or parody, performance or video involvement, licensing, and types of royalties. Whether your particular use qualifies is your responsibility to investigate.

Perform parodies live, delivering in person, or record them, if you so choose. An instrumental track often becomes the foundation. Can't find the appropriate instrumental? Try Sound Cloud or YouTube. Ask those you may know in the recording or radio industry. Don't know anyone? Well, that's what Internet communities are for on LinkedIn, Facebook or other sites.

Use karaoke tracks if you're willing to absorb any added cost. If you can play the song using your own guitar, piano or other instruments, you can record your own backing track before you lay down the vocals. This helps you to have your verses and choruses in just the right places.

Payment Concerns

Songwriter's Market, published annually, can guide your creative energies and payment needs as you establish pricing. Songwriters earn their payment through three major income streams: mechanical royalties, performance royalties, and synch fees, according to Nashville Songwriters Association International.

The rules and regulations can be very different than those of the average freelance writer, whose livelihood is the prevue of this particular book. For those specifics, consult resources and websites listed in the back of this book.

Seven

You've Got This

*You can. You should. And if you're
brave enough to start, you will.*
— Stephen King, author

We're not quite finished exploring this first set of writing avenues—a few better suited and more available for some of you than others—but regardless if you take two or two dozen of the money-making ideas presented in this book, every writer needs what this chapter offers.

Taking care of your creative side enhances your existing business and financial goals. If you're already a business owner or you work in a helping field, you know the value of self-care, forecasting ahead, and making use of down time. Either way, these pages may refresh that knowledge.

This chapter's topics should help organize your thoughts and life so that whatever forms of writing you delve into, in a primary career, small business, or alternative income stream, you have an awareness of your strengths and weaknesses.

Much rides on knowing yourself. If you're too confident when there's some remedial work to be done, you may likely stumble. Ask any writer or author who has put work out there before it was ready to truly be consumed. On the other hand, if you commit to too much, full bore ahead without a plan, that may trip you up as well.

Every writer needs a confidence boost to the creative spirit. It's vital to coping through rejection and dry spells, both of which will inevitably hit. These pages will also outline some key nuances of the writing world, that is, realistic expectations. But before we get into that, let's start with a few more you-can-do-it-too stories to cheerlead you forward.

Searching for Magic

While the publishing world has changed the level of encouragement that writers crave has not. Many prolific authors who have become household names started their craft without cellphones, Internet research, eBooks, and social media. Think it's hard now to attract work and then a following? Veteran writers had it much harder.

When I began my freelance career, mall bookstores were common as were trips to the library to use...get this, the card catalog. Writers bought or sent away for physical copies of sample magazines. I remember the sheer elation when Borders Books & Music housed the largest selection of published works and how the staff actually got quizzed on book knowledge, a prerequisite to being hired.

Twenty years prior, Doubleday published Stephen King's *Carrie* in 1974, but only after King had written stories for magazines while he toiled in a mill, a laundry and at a school. He had grown so frustrated with his literary efforts that he tossed manuscript pages into the trash. If his wife had not rescued those crumpled pages, King recounted in his memoir, that first book, as well as his career, may not have begun when it did.

Anna Quindlen began as a part-time reporter for the *New York Post* during this era. She would go on to join *The New York Times,* become a columnist for that paper plus *Newsweek,* before she left in 1995 to write novels.

Line up two dozen successful writers, and I'm going to bet that the majority—maybe all of them—heard encouragement that landed softly in their hearts. Most likely one individual or a few people said, "I think you've got something here."

Those, folks, are magic words! Like food and water those words nourish the creative soul. If a cool breeze refreshes most people, that phrase allows writers to exhale with a satisfied smile.

It means so much because writing is a fairly solitary endeavor upon which much self-doubt gets cast.

While novel writing is the stuff to which introverts are often drawn, extroverts tend to prefer journalistic, investigative writing. But at one time or another, most writers separate themselves, even if it's with ear buds in a crowded coffee shop or newsroom. Rest assured, they will surface among others when they need connection and certainly when they desire feedback on their prose. That solitary toiling, however, takes its toll. Perseverative thought will veer to negative self-talk if we let it. An aversion to risk taking may be another side effect of solitary confinement.

For that, however, I'm going to quote a prolific Maryland novelist named Nora Roberts. "If you don't go after what you want, you'll never have it," Nora has been known to say. "If you don't ask, the answer is always no. If you don't step forward, you're always in the same place."

A Writer's Idiosyncrasies & Imperatives

How many stacks of printed stuff—clippings, magazines to be read, journal articles you think you might use—sit on your end tables and counter tops? Yes, I thought so!

When I referenced this writer's quirk in workshops, people would chuckle. I tend to think that clipping, filing, and thinking about how you will use that material and research are constant writer pursuits. These habits spark your inner muse. After all, a writer is what she perceives on a future page.

That said, if your background—the place where you live and work—rivals the B-roll of a reality TV hoarding episode, then I won't legitimize total chaos either. There are writers who lack organizational abilities and undermine themselves. Don't let that become you. Most of us do gather a few piles of written material that "we just might need" when we're in writing mode. We yearn for the rainy afternoon to tackle it. You have to be the judge of whether your journalistic stash helps or hinders. The same choices exist for you to mismanage your schedule and squander writing time for less productive pursuits. Enter social media.

It takes some discipline and self-determination to pull back from popular trends, but you likely realize the sheer time zap you enter into when spending too much time online. You get nothing written. Lack of keystrokes causes hastily drafted copy or no written material at all. Nothing created leads to zero balance in the checking account after bills surface. Develop the business acumen to retreat from those things that keep your goals on a forward trajectory.

The not-so news flash is that we writers get distracted. Something catches our fancy and we're off researching it, and before you know it, another hour has crept by. Authors Gary Keller and Jay Papasan use proverbs, quotes, and a movie skit to introduce the productivity-enhancing advice they extrapolate in *The One Thing*. Success, they report, scatters when your concentration shifts and wanes from the one thing you really care to accomplish. Living a less complex life, with fewer interruptions, whistles and bells, helps to that end.

When You Have Something Good

Just after someone tells you that your something special warrants a wider audience, self-confidence may disappear as quickly as it bolstered you. Writers may rationalize their hesitancy to become published by reminding themselves that they have never gone down that path before, it's uncertain, and the destination could be quite a way off. All of that is true.

To counter that notion, I'll quote another author who was quite popular when I began in publishing. Author and speaker Tom Peters said, "If a window of opportunity appears, don't pull down the shade."

Allow sunshine and positivity through your windows with the energy it all creates. Persevere with gratitude and humility. Be thankful that you get to wake up and enjoy what you do each day with a passion that others in your peer set may not have when the alarm sounds each morning. If you've come to this crossroads with a modicum of talent and a whole lot of instant success, lose the ego or the realities of publishing may lose it for you.

Occasionally writers are in the enviable position that an editor or publisher has actually approached them first, asked to see their story and plunked down lots of dollar bills so that they may take the time to create...and produce. It's the chair time, the blank pages, and the blinking cursor that nags most of us in this field.

I have never truly believed in writer's block. It makes for a cute Snoopy cartoon, not much more. Right after a rejection, you may momentarily wish to chuck the writing life for summersaults in a circus tent or septic tank clean out. You may even rationalize to yourself that you could end up more famous or wealthier in either of those pursuits. Well, that's not why you got this book.

On those days when you lack the motivation to write, do some other task that's productive. Several exist. Here are a few:

- Assemble your published clips or Internet links of proven work. If you've saved copies of your published work, which you always should, assemble these into both a physical and visually pleasing collection as well as an online document with hyperlinks or frames that pop open with evidence of your best output.

- Always—this is important—print out pleasing copies of online contributions just in case there's a day you can no longer access your published work via the links to it.

- Work on LinkedIn or another social media presence.

- Follow-up on telephone calls or emails that expand your network. Check on submissions you've sent as well.

- Conduct research for pending projects. This steers you ahead, leading to additional ideas and eventual acceptances.

- Interview new sources or put out requests for experts. Reach out to book publishing publicity departments for contact information regarding authors who have done research that you can tap into and cite properly.

The average writer's path requires the personality traits of discipline, patience, and tenacity. You'll probably want to argue the merits of your work at some point in your career. It's inevitable but try not to. You may need the good wishes or referral of your editor someday.

That editor could move to another publication so swallow this temptation and try to learn from constructive criticism. Use your perseverance to write every day, even when it means doing a complete rewrite of what you accomplished prior. Resist marrying your prose.

When editors do comment, be gracious and appreciative that they offered you something. Trust me: plenty of people in this industry never get to offer guidance because hectic workdays interfere. Consider it fantastic if they do. Work to be the writer who masters the craft, ultimately who needs little editing, yet remains open to whatever feedback and edits are requested.

Some projects will seem like a chore, but the more you commit pen to paper (or fingers to keyboard), the better writer you'll become with a solid output ethic and on-time delivery. Nothing replaces parking your butt in the chair and just getting to the keyboard.

Bouncing Back From "No Thanks"

Once manuscripts have been sent into cyberspace or the postal service, patience is a virtue. Waiting and wondering, even for the dreaded word "no" torments many writers.

Just as you parked it in the chair to create, get out of it now to celebrate (temporarily) a job well done with time earned for some self-care. This clears the creative mind so that you form new ideas, replenish energy, and refocus your mind.

What you choose could be a weekend off, a vacation, an outing or merely a few hours to do anything else but writing. Engaging in other imaginative endeavors, whether it's cooking, gardening, art, or decorating, often meets an inherent need for creativity while refreshing the mind, body and spirit.

Spend time with family and friends. Take a trip, catch up on an improvement project (e.g., reorganize a closet) or put together a puzzle or tiny plastic bricks with the children...maybe alone.

Then, park yourself back in place to churn out the next project. Hopefully, you can soon do another little dance or lift a glass in toast upon article acceptance or project go-ahead. However, if rejection is your lot in today's work life, own it as an ordinary occurrence, then learn from it.

John Grisham withstood rejection letters from sixteen agents and more than thirty publishing houses before his first book got published. After college, law school and representing clients in court, Grisham spent sixty- to eighty-hour workweeks as a Mississippi state legislator. He rose an hour earlier than he normally would have to carve out time to write his first novel *A Time to Kill.*

After a series of rejections, once he landed an agent the turn-down cycle started all over again with publishers. Bill Thompson, the editor who discovered Stephen King (who had his own climb) gave Grisham a limited 5,000 book run and a $15,000 advance.

In this next sentence, you may expect me to write that Grisham gave up passing legislation for plots and characters. Not quite. None of this, including his self-styled book tour, did much more than add extra fans and bookstore owners into his network. The sale, however, inspired John Grisham to keep at his craft. Does this sound like vaguely familiar advice? Indeed, I have stated in all of my writing books, an initial sale boosts self-esteem and bank balances to propel writers down more profitable paths. Anticipate that when you take two steps forward, you might take one right back.

Before the House of the Mouse

Walt Disney, an apprentice cartoonist at a Kansas City newspaper, gambled that he could produce newsreel spoofs, animated fairy tales and instructional films. When he had already given up his apartment to sleep at the office and kindly accepted free meals at restaurants, his sole client's bankruptcy hit him hard.

Walt left the Midwest to join his brother Roy in California with only $40 from the sale of his camera. They teamed with others for a new take on *Alice in Wonderland.* That didn't quite work as they had planned.

Enter a rabbit named Oswald, whose film presence bankrolled marriage, a home purchase and satisfying work, that is, until two New York film distributors, instrumental in Walt's big break, demanded concessions. They also presented an ultimatum to join their staff and announced that the rights to Oswald the Rabbit were indeed licensed under the film distributors' names.

In one fell swoop, the Disney brothers lost their business and artistic creation. Out of desperation, they created a mouse dressed in red velvet pants named Mortimer. Mrs. Disney disliked that name and suggested Mickey, a less pretentious one. *Steamboat Willie*, featuring said mouse, attracted press coverage and new distributors as fast as it spawned Donald, Daisy, Goofy and Pluto.

Older and wiser, Walt Disney maintained artistic control and the rights to his characters.

Just as Disney learned from mistakes and set ego aside to accept suggestions on a better name, you also can learn something from most every setback and opinion. Editors reject manuscripts and queries for many reasons. Perhaps another writer beat you to the editor's desk with the same idea or a staff writer got assigned to it.

Should you see your idea published in next month's magazine, know that what you just read took months to appear in print. Chalk it up to coincidence.

At the same time, ask yourself if your query was targeted enough, whether it supported the readership or advertisers' needs. As separate as the editorial and advertising departments try to claim, advertising pays for magazines. If your idea supports existing or future ads, it stands a better chance of being published.

Self-Care Eases Bumps Through Pot Holes

Writers face rejection, some more than others. Certainly, on the days where it rises to depressive proportions—and frankly even when it's a minor player in your life—you must implement self-care strategies.

The concept here means a healthy focus upon self so that you do not sacrifice mind, body and soul to your publishing goals. You can achieve this as you:

Surround yourself with a support system. These people will complement and grasp your creative energies. It's trickier than it seems. Let's say loved ones measure on-the-job productivity by numbers and billable hours. Their sense of validation in their work and your triumph at finishing a feature that may not see print for months may be at ends of the spectrum. Opposites do attract, however, and discussing these differences in motivation, process, and outcome openly creates understanding.

Reroute rejected material to other markets. Limited rejections won't stifle your career. Move on from them, for if you don't, you'll miss a sale that awaits you.

Hold back from publishing your first book. Write the sequel and maybe other books if you plan a trilogy. This was the advice I learned from best-selling author Sylvia Day when I heard her speak at a conference. It does make sense. Stick with the writing process to keep you learning and growing. Otherwise, those tasks could get sidetracked.

Exercise away writing blues. These regular breaks ward off worries and improve circulation to the brain, making it perhaps a bit more available to your brainstorming and ideas. Exercise does your body and imaginative abilities a huge favor as feel-good chemicals course through your bloodstream.

Change your atmosphere. If the budget allows for a quick getaway or day trip, take one. If not, do your research at a favorite bookstore. Surrounded by books, I feel at home and my writer's brain finds its happy place. Take your laptop to the library or local coffee shop. Alternate between tea, decaf and regular coffee since too much caffeine may plummet your productivity later. Take a scenery break for a new coping mechanism. Doing things for and with other people provides an altruistic boost to them and to you.

Practice mindfulness. The ability to live in the moment with what matters helps us to unplug from gadgetry and slow our minds and bodies, away from cognitive overload. Multi-tasking may work for short spurts; over time, however, it makes us more susceptible to stress.

Get enough rest. A study from Brigham and Women's Hospital tracked the sleep patterns of Harvard students for thirty days, comparing academic performance. The findings: those with irregular sleep patterns, that is not having the same schedule of being asleep, interrupted their circadian rhythms or body clock. This regulates melatonin, a hormone that helps us to fall asleep and remain asleep. Fluctuating bedtimes and waking up at different hours is not optimal for our bodies and minds.

Soak in natural light as you position your workspace accordingly. Couple sunlight with exercise and mindfulness and you have a very healthy trifecta going here.

Keep in touch with colleagues and friends if the work becomes too solitary. Writing is intensely introspective. Camaraderie buffers those negative responses so that you don't take them too personally.

Read voraciously. Make this a priority. "Reading is the creative center of a writer's life," writes Stephen King in *On*

Writing: A Memoir of the Craft. It sure is. I've never met a writer who doesn't benefit from reading. Thus, treat yourself to a morning or afternoon at your favorite bookstore, someplace that has a substantial newsstand, or even the library. Probably a good idea to do this alone since loved ones know how writers get absorbed in reading material. Get into the habit of carrying a book with you for idle moments, crack the covers of one before opting for television, and be sure to download one or several apps for Kindle, Nook or iBooks on your smartphone or tablet.

Put Your Best Thinking Forward

When negative self-talk becomes never-ending with pessimistic predictions or fears, it's time to use what we therapists call cognitive-behavioral therapy (CBT). Yes, you can do this.

If you're really in a mental rut, a few counseling sessions with a licensed therapist may surely help. In my role as such, I often describe myself as a thinking partner, particularly to young children, adolescents, or those reluctant to reach out for help. Seeking help can be reframed as a sign of strength. Furthermore, if I teach CBT well enough to clients, they learn to work with their thoughts and behaviors almost daily when stress arises.

Let me show you how. Write down your automatic thought— that notion that pops uneasily into your head and you can't shake it from getting you worried or upset. We'll get to it in just a moment, but first an example.

Let's say José wakes up on his day off from a full-time job poised to produce financial queries for the consumer editor who often contracts his work. Then, he retrieves the morning mail.

"Dammit," he yells. "I should have suggested two ideas and seen this coming." He shook his head. "I'm such an idiot always screwing up."

José reads his editor's few sentences, hand scrawled on magazine letterhead. It reads:

"Your proposed idea on social justice could work, José, but we decided at the last meeting to go with end-of-year tax strategies after the latest stock market slide rather than a charitable giving/tax deduction round up. I'd like to reconsider this perhaps for next November. Nudge me in April, if you don't mind. All the best — Leonard."

What's more when the next magazine issue comes, José feels down on himself once again. He mutters, "This looks a little similar to something I proposed to Leonard. I'll bet he ripped off my idea." José tosses the magazines onto his table. "Besides, they must not like me. Took them long enough to get up with me."

José silently convinces himself, once again, that new writers have no chance of getting published. Without ever checking out his beliefs, José becomes one of those writers who gives up because of self-esteem issues and wayward thoughts.

Fix Your Thoughts, Improve Your Future

Lists of cognitive thinking errors crop up via Google searches and in books. You spent money on this one; thus, wearing my therapy hat, I'll save you the trouble with my own list.

Briefly scan this. Where do you think José's thoughts get trapped? When you think you have some ideas continue reading.

Okay, ready? José's cognitive stumbling blocks could be:

- Seeing things all one way or the polar opposite (no grey)
- Overgeneralizing with words like always and never
- Predicting the future to a negative outcome
- Jumping ahead to poor conclusions
- Taking things personally
- Holding himself responsible for things out of his control
- Labeling himself or anyone else with global assessments
- Imposing self-pressure (should-, must- or ought-to)
- Allowing one thing to make everything else seem bad
- Discounting positives and looking through a bleak filter
- Blaming others while ignoring his own responsibility
- Running with emotions rather than fact
- Convincing himself of what is not true

We have all likely gotten our brains stuck in some of these traps. Yet occasionally, we revisit the same thinking errors more than others.

José committed a number of these cognitive mistakes. He had some *all or nothing thinking* going on and *overgeneralized* with a word such as *always*. José *took personally* the rejection, and he *labeled* himself as well as all new writers when he engaged in some *fortune telling* about his or their chances of success. When José uttered the word *should*, he placed *should/must/ought to* pressures upon himself, and he *discounted the positive* that Leonard, his editor, wanted to hear from him again.

Using a little CBT, José could remember times when plenty of his ideas have been used in this publication. Aaron Beck, a cognitive therapy pioneer, encouraged people to check out the evidence for their faulty thoughts.

If this type of thinking become a way of life, not merely an occurrence, it's a bigger problem. Return to your automatic thought that you wrote down, then review this list of common cognitive errors. Very likely, you may not find any supportive evidence to back your original, faulty thoughts. Can you spot when you veer into these traps?

Adjust your thinking. You can only change yourself, your perceptions, and your actions. Albert Ellis, another contributor to cognitive therapy, posited that much of what we get worked up about, turns out to be our irrational beliefs. Our job is to dispute those in what Ellis dubbed his ABCD model. There is an activating event, a belief, and a consequence. We must dispute any irrational beliefs.

CBT is highly evidence-based. Work on your thoughts and behavior—that is, force yourself into new productive and healthy habits when old ones cease to help—and this should ultimately improve your outlook.

If you're highly anxious or down in the dumps (especially more than two weeks straight), you may need to couple this approach with interventions such as therapy and medication (again not the purview of this book). However, if you do combine treatments, the effectiveness rate soars to the high nineties.

Are Writers Moodier Than Others?

Dr. Kay Jamison, a well-known psychologist and researcher at Johns Hopkins, as well as the author of *Touched with Fire*, studied creative types looking into mental health and seasonal patterns of mood and productivity. She found that many artists and writers noted changes in their sleep just prior to intensely creative episodes.

Twenty-eight percent described spontaneous waking at three to four in the morning, being unable to return to sleep. Fifty percent reported a sharp mood increase just prior to intense creativity, describing themselves as elated, excited, with anticipatory energy, sometimes even euphoric or ecstatic.

Still others expressed more anxiety, isolation, low ebb, gloominess, despair, sexual pressure, restlessness and dissatisfaction at other points in their lives. Many also showed clear peaks of productivity in spring and in fall, thus manifesting a seasonal component to their creativity.

Anecdotally, the writing life has more than its share of ups and downs. Thus, it's another reason I devote focus not only to bank balances, but also self-esteem and confidence building.

Writing as the Ultimate Cathartic Outlet

I would be remiss if I didn't add that writing can sometimes open old emotional baggage or it can take us places we would much rather have detoured. After I wrote *Surviving Separation and Divorce,* which is a woman's guide to recovering from that tough time in her life, people asked if writing that book healed me. No, I would answer. To help others I had to be at a good place myself.

Revisiting memories or experiences, even when they belong to interviewees, may drain any writer. I will admit that while I love my counseling practice, hearing people's concerns by day and writing serious non-fiction at night drove me to write women's fiction under my pen name Lauren Monroe. Though it was still work, it felt less depleting. I could create fun, character banter, romance, and satisfying endings. I controlled the dramas rather than traumas having too much control over me.

Yet I can reframe (another CBT technique) my own earlier divorce impact, unnecessary legal issues and even passive-aggressive people I've encountered because my non-fiction titles have helped countless readers. Would I have written about these topics had my life gone in different directions?

I used my strengths, teaching skills, and knowledge of human behavior to inform both my non-fiction and my novelist creations. What's more, friends and colleagues have reported that some of my best work stemmed from projects where I have had a personal connection to the topic and a passion to help others avoid or overcome similar struggles.

My examples are rather ordinary. Famous celebrities and poignant authors have done the same. Maya Angelou and Oprah Winfrey come to mind for they both survived hardship. A certain level of giveback has been evident in their life work.

Angelou, the late, renowned poet, experienced frequent indignities and the trauma of rape as a young girl. Her testimony helped to convict her attacker, who when released from prison was immediately beaten to death by family. This shocked Maya into silence as she felt that if she spoke to anyone else, that person would suffer the same fate. A schoolteacher intervened, gently aiding Maya out of muteness with poetry and the beauty of words spoken aloud.

Books had always been a source of strength, but coupled with this unconditional positive regard, Maya Angelou wouldn't be reduced by what she had endured. Her writing symbolized reinvention, with heartache and triumph that became art and a celebration of life itself. Her 1969 memoir *I Know Why the Caged Bird Sings* became the first non-fiction best-selling book by an African-American woman. Awards and honors continued until her passing in 2014. President Barack Obama called Ms. Angelou "a brilliant writer, a fierce friend, and a truly phenomenal woman."

Oprah also bounced between homes. She suffered assaults, rebelled as a teen (almost landing in juvenile services), and ended up redirecting her life, intelligence and personality to study broadcast journalism. She got a part-time job reporting TV news, but left college at nineteen when an anchor spot opened in Nashville. Years later, a Baltimore station offered more exposure.

Things fell apart, however, with an on-camera image that management didn't think quite fit. Rather than break her contract, they gave her an afternoon talk show. I think you know how this all turned out, but just in case, within a few years, a Chicago TV station courted Oprah for *AM Chicago* where her frank, sometimes humorous appeal, grabbed the number one talk show spot. It was nationally syndicated in 1985, and today, Oprah owns OWN, a network bearing her initials.

The Good & Bad of Bragging Rights

Throughout this book, I have tried to include inspiration from those you might recognize as household names as well as individuals who have succeeded though not to stardom. At least not yet! Some days it may seem as though you'll never get very far. Highlight this: Believe that you can.

When people find out you're a writer, the revelation turns heads and invites curiosity. It's rather cool to have a writer friend. People want to know where you get your material. They blush having read your sex scenes, if you write any. When you're tremendously lucky, these long-time supporters or random new fans become part of your "street team" designed to alert the world through word-of-mouth sales and social media sharing. It's easy to feel confident in these moments.

Of course, writers face unfortunate stereotypes, too. We're all wealthy, raking in royalties, and it's such an ease of effort to plunk out the next article, project or book. Ah, no. The vast majority of writers work their behinds off and most work to pay the bills like everyone else.

People's quick judgments can actually hinder writers who wish to make a modest wage or merely extra income. Some folks might assume your work is widely distributed, therefore, why should they bother posting a book review or sharing anything from your Facebook page? If people pull down a salary (with benefits), they may have no clue what the creative struggle let alone some paychecks or the waiting for one looks like. Furthermore, they might grow resentful if you have achieved milestones they would have liked in their own lives or careers. Much of this gets based upon faulty assumption.

All or any of this can send your self-worth south when you aren't at those writing life peaks. Worse yet: you encounter judgment if, heaven forbid, you promote your own projects.

Keisha, a writer told me how she felt judged by a friend, whom we'll call Zarah, employed in a highly compensated, secure field. Keisha thought Zarah understood the vast differences in their work lives—Zarah being left logical and scientific compared with her own right, creative brain and a career based upon projects and flexible hours (the same for pay).

As a writer, Keisha sent infrequent alerts to her contact list when a special opportunity existed to enjoy her work. She did this maybe once a quarter or every four or five months, perhaps.

One day, Zarah chastised Keisha for "commercializing" their friendship, having squirmed at being told that Keish's play was being produced locally and when tickets would be on sale.

I tackle promotion later in this book, but I'll add here that you need not guilt yourself if you self-promote your work. People have varying tolerances, but unless all you communicate is business-driven, I don't think it's a sin to alert others about your writing output and the opportunities to enjoy it.

That said, if you know of someone who gets twitchy or easily put off, distance such matters from them. Use an ounce of savvy and a big helping of common sense. Occasional updates have been known to turn dormant clients into active ones as the gesture conveys a willingness to work together again and healthy self-confidence in what you do.

Connect with your fan base, especially if you create actual products. In a Facebook group or LinkedIn community, post a good amount of non-sales graphics and news related to your field. Focus upon easy-to-agree-with material that steers clear of strong, polarized opinion. One author regularly shares silly animal posts, outdoor photography, and inspiring quotes.

On my women's fiction novel page, Lauren Monroe (my alter ego or pen name for fiction) shares Chesapeake imagery and tips on traveling to this area, as it's the setting of a series.

I also add reputable relationship findings, positive sayings, interspersed with graphic images I've created to provide glimpses into my characters' lives and novel content. Yes, I post sales info, too, because everyone likes a bargain. If my eBooks are discounted, readers can save money or gift to a friend. When I'm running a holiday event, people can't come if they don't know about it. Overall, I aim to keep my posts fun and light.

The bottom line: don't expect others to believe in you if you don't believe in your own efforts. Most businesspeople respect a can-do attitude. *Please* and *thank you* are valuable words so if someone has posted favorable comments or given you a LinkedIn referral, be sure to acknowledge it.

Cheerleading When You Need It Most

Whether it's your own faulty reasoning, others' snap judgments or hours spent pounding out prose into a keyboard, writing is lonely. It can grate on even an introvert's nerves some days.

For that reason—and many more—I suggest that you build what I call an encouragement file. Fill it with items such as a copy of your first check, first published clipping or sale, letters or email messages from readers your work touched enough that they let you know about it. You get the idea.

Trust me; you will need the pick-me-up. At that moment, reach into your file and be affirmed that you can make it through the rest of the day, the creative dry spell or slump. Know that where you are today is not where you will be in another week, month, or a year or two from now.

To emotionally survive and thrive as a writer, hang around positive people who believe in your goals. Fellow writers understand the artistic life, but no matter whom you consider your best buds, I hope that they bestow a hefty dose of validation when you need it the most. It's also on you to get up out of your chair, move around, take a walk in the sunshine and use a little of that CBT I discussed earlier. An overwhelming majority of people I polled in my research said they experienced the normal ups and downs plus ordinary worries just like any other professional. You will feel this. That, I can almost guarantee. Interestingly enough, an even greater majority in my informal survey shared that without their writing, they would feel incomplete and unsatisfied.

You Really Do Have This

When I taught my then classroom-based workshop, I began with first-name introductions and a brief sentence about goals—what did students want to get out of the workshop?

One student wasn't sure how she could make a difference. As it turned out, she worked in the bakery at the large grocery chain we all shopped in, within the Pittsburgh area. Seeing her quizzical look, I said. "You have so much to offer. Tons of editors need holiday baking tips or kid-friendly party ideas for weary parents."

Shore Thing Publishing
PROOF COPY

I reiterated to my students that each one of them knew something substantially more than other people, who probably yearned to learn what they already knew. I found out later that this one particular student, the baker, had almost dropped out of class, but as she reflected upon the lecture that day, she returned the following week.

She shared that she had left class that first day with six different article and filler ideas. She stayed the course—literally!

That's what I urge you to do.

Eight

Solo Success Strategies

Wealth is not about having a lot of money;
it's about having a lot of options.
— Chris Rock, comedian

S ince many writers will embark on their freelance efforts from the comforts of their own homes, I will discuss how to carve out your workspace, set up a home office, as well as some important business protocols to help you to squirrel away necessary funds, again with the priority number one goal of keeping the income you do earn.

This chapter will also address how to avoid chaos and disorganization with its cost of time/money. Furthermore, it may counterbalance any remaining hesitancy or fears you have about starting out.

The Ideal Office Myth

I have had a variety of workspaces—from small corners of a condominium or large room, furnished basement offices, upstairs bedrooms converted for work and out-of-the home offices, which served primarily for a private practice but could also become a place to create, edit my writing, and meet with colleagues.

Unfortunately, I've experienced the consequences of spaces that upon first set-up I had thought were ideal but later rationalized reasons why I should take my red pen or laptop someplace else.

In the winter, I had deemed my basement office too chilly; then, I had to remediate for radon forcing me out until the project was completed. Other days, I told myself that I'd benefit from more direct sunlight. Still, too, there were days I felt too lazy to move out of a comfy sofa or bed when the muse struck with my morning coffee. One time *that* landed me in the hospital emergency department with back spasms, hardly helpful to my productivity goals. Trust me when I say that muscle relaxers do not spark the creative muse.

Propping up poorly with a laptop caused that for sure. What my physical therapist and I jokingly called "mouse arm" later led to neck, shoulder and arm issues from sitting too long without sufficient movement breaks. I don't mean to sound like a certifiable mess. Fortunately, I learned better habits.

Each writer has to decide what space works best given what's available. Most consider a separate room with ample shelves, file drawers, worktop, computer, printer, comfortable chair, and some sunlight to be ideal. If you must function in less than ideal, so be it. Mind over matter, you can still achieve a lot.

Already covered sufficiently, writers are what they produce. Parking it somewhere to create is priority number one. Let priority number two be that you work to live, not to harm your physical or mental health, and certainly not to shorten your life from too much time spent at the keyboard...or spent there incorrectly. Pay attention to ergonomics, that is, where you position your monitor, computer keyboard, desk chair and other parts of your workstation.

Your Health Is at Risk

Think I'm exaggerating? *The Washington Post* ran "The Health Hazards of Sitting" in January 2014 with a startling but very informational graphic headlined "Don't Just Sit There!" It outlined the maladies one suffers relegating the body to a sedentary job and made specific recommendations to improve your ergonomics and posture. Indeed, sitting six or more hours a day makes us forty percent more likely to face health problems.

If that doesn't cause you to take notice, read on. The *Annals of Internal Medicine* published a review of research in 2015 that reported the hazards were greatest for those people who sat eight or nine hours a day, and even worse for those who did not exercise regularly. Spelled out it points to higher cardiovascular, cancer and diabetic risks.

The American College of Sports Medicine advocates that each of us gets at minimum thirty minutes of moderate activity daily in addition to merely getting up and moving around throughout the day. In a brochure, the organization points to how sitting impairs the body's ability to properly deposit fat from the blood stream, and when it cannot, the elevated blood fats become a risk factor for heart disease. With a sedentary lifestyle, our HDL (healthy cholesterol) cannot clean up the plaque, which sticks to our arteries. This can lead to mortality if left unchecked.

Okay, those are the most serious health risks of a writer's sedentary lifestyle, but also vexing is the tendency for us writers to experience postural ailments, such as carpal tunnel syndrome and back problems. If you're already suffering with soreness and pain, check with your physician first. To ward off orthopedic problems, *WebMD* offers several wrist exercises to prevent carpal tunnel syndrome as well as back and core strengthening exercises.

Sometimes, investing in a half-size foam roller that accommodates your torso to lie on, along with simple dumbbell weights, provides you an on-the-floor stretching break that opens up those tight shoulders and arms. After those anecdotes I shared, I now lay on the roller, stretching my arms like a goal post, a two- or three-pound weight in each hand. I can feel the stretch.

Another simple maneuver is the overhead arm extension where you reach high, palms up, interlace your fingers, and gently push up a few times. Always, consult your physician or a fitness trainer if you have concerns regarding your stretching and exercise routines.

Health Insurance Options

Everyone needs health insurance because a freak accident, in addition to ordinary illness or body wear and tear, can wreak havoc, literally, on your bank account.

Unless you work as a staff writer earning a paycheck with payroll deductions for health, disability, and life insurance—and perhaps even when you do—saving money on health-related matters makes personal and financial sense. Tap into the following to defray costs:

- Other employment coverage, a spouse's job benefits, or COBRA (the Consolidated Omnibus Budget Reconciliation Act) when you leave a job with healthcare benefits. Often employer-based plans offer more comprehensive coverage with lower deductibles and member responsibility than individual policies.

- The Affordable Care Act, passed by the 111th U.S. Congress and signed into law in March 2010, afforded coverage for people who may have been declined previous insurance due to pre-existing conditions. It set up exchanges where consumers could compare and choose between healthcare plans. As of this writing, that's all changing at a time when baby boomers age with more physical needs and employers encourage part-time work so as to reduce employee health benefits.

- Find group coverage through a local Chamber of Commerce, a large national group such as the American Association of Retired People (AARP), or a professional organization such as the American Society of Journalists and Authors, Author's Guild, the Editorial Freelance Association, Freelancer's Union, and the Society of Children's Book Writers & Illustrators. Some college alumni associations, certain memberships or warehouse clubs may be large enough to offer pooled coverage. See this book's resources as well for ideas.

- Save on expenses with a healthy diet and exercise, get good sleep, and follow safety protocols. If you can afford to pay cash, you might try negotiating private-pay rates with healthcare providers. For minor illnesses, stitches or lab tests, it's less costly to see a primary care physician or urgent clinic rather than use a hospital emergency department.

- Go with generic drugs whenever possible. If not, ask for pharmaceutical samples or search online for co-pay cards that lessen the cost of newer medications. Counseling services can sometimes be rendered on a sliding scale, at a community mental health agency, or a practice where graduate social workers, counselors or marriage/family therapists obtain hours toward licensure while they work under the clinical supervision of a fully licensed mental health professional. Psychologists operate similarly.

- Establish a Health Savings Account (HSA) offered through employers, financial institutions, or insurance companies, especially when there are high-deductible plans. With an HSA, you contribute pre-tax dollars up to a certain threshold to pay for qualified medical, vision, or dental expenses now or in the future.
- Look to major insurance companies for quotes on disability and life insurance. Again, professional organizations and most of the other options mentioned for healthcare may offer other types of insurance policies.
- If you encounter a severe disability but have paid self-employment taxes into the Social Security Administration, check the number of credits you have (years paid into the system). Your credits only qualify you part of the way. Your disability would have to be approved. Expect a lot of appointments and paperwork with outside parties before you are approved in order to determine the true amount of any benefits you might receive.
- Always keep careful records and receipts for HSA or flexible spending reimbursement, tax records or planning for the benefit years ahead.

Set Aside Necessary Funds

We've covered health and insurances but there's still retirement, tax withholding and just plain savings. Most freelance writers need to regularly set aside funds for these purposes as well as for emergency expenditures. You know, when the HVAC system breaks down or your computer crashes to the point of no return.

Precisely how you do this is not the purview of this book. Experts encourage most anyone to set aside six to twelve months of living expenses to cover them for loss of income or some sudden emergency. For the self-employed, that estimate doubles.

According to the Internal Revenue Service (IRS) website, individuals who expect to owe tax of $1,000 or more when they file their return should pay estimated tax; for small corporations expecting to owe $500 or more in tax, they should also. IRS Form 1040-ES helps you to figure your estimated tax responsibility and contains instructions on paying it.

If you have a staff job with an employer-sponsored 401(k) or similar retirement vehicle, you're ahead of the game here, yet when you earn income from even a side business, stashing away extra retirement funds secures your long-term future.

Simplified Employee Pension (SEP) plans function much like a 40(k), only they are designed for self-employed individuals and small businesses. They offer tax-deferred savings now when you file your returns, and you pay tax later upon withdrawing the accumulated assets. Like any other retirement instrument, SEP IRAs are subject to Required Minimum Distributions shortly after you turn 70 years old.

You may also wish to look into a solo or individual 401(k). For 2016, employees were allowed to divert up to $18,000 of their income and an additional $6,000 if they were more than fifty years old. The employer side of a solo 401(k) contribution was limited to twenty-five percent of one's total business income for the year. Generally, as of this writing, this type of account allows individuals to stash away more retirement funds than the SEP plans, and up to fifty percent of the total value is permitted (up to $50,000) as an individual 401(k) loan. Always discuss your circumstances with a qualified tax planner well before the end of each year.

Once again, tax revisions get enacted and periodic updates occur which make the tax landscape an ever-evolving business dilemma. Be sure to consult the proper professionals before you make big decisions about your finances moving forward.

Working at Home

Today, many people have great rooms, enough space to convert a nook into a writing space. Gone are the days when only separate rooms could be used as a tax-deductible home office expense. Thus, sections of bedrooms, dens, kitchens or family rooms may help you to lower your net income with home office expense.

Some self-employed people frown upon taking that deduction even when they are entitled to it for fear it will raise audit risk. Today, large numbers of people telework or have home-based businesses, but you must feel comfortable with your choice. Maintain proof of your workspace with photos and other data in the unlikely event you need to substantiate your deduction.

An accordion door provides one way to section off a room portion; it will hide your stacks of creativity lurking within. Build desks and shelving into walls or install recessed lights so that other fixtures don't take up valuable space. I've also seen sections of countertop secured on top of file cabinets that offer more of a flat surface than traditional desks one might purchase.

Some writers living in small quarters turn to freestanding units (much like an armoire), available at furniture or office stores with just enough room for computer equipment, a peripheral item, and everything in one spot. You can make a small space feel much larger with lighter off-white or pastel colors. Halogen and fluorescent bulbs produce more light, last longer, and use less energy. Task lighting is also efficient.

Lower Expenses Yield Higher Income

To research this book, I surveyed dozens of writers—novelists, non-fiction writers, poets and others. Nearly sixty percent reported that they would spend money on books, magazines, memberships, travel and technology, within reason of course, because they saw these expenses as necessary to doing business as a writer.

Fifty percent said they would spend some money to network and socialize with other creative types who understood them and their work.

At the same time, twenty-seven percent admitted they would attend more virtual writing events in order to eliminate the costs of travel and food. Half of those polled said they used the library, purchased used books as well as discounted eBooks to trim their business expenses.

Like most taxpayers, each year you review expenses you have incurred and how much net profit your writing has earned. Clearly, cutting costs yields more disposable income. Here are a few tips I've gleaned over the years for writers to slash expenses:

- Ask suppliers, stores, and health clubs to offer business discounts of at least ten percent, and to allow this discount on top of advertised specials. If you teach or take classes, ask for educational discounts. Over age fifty-five or sixty-five? You may qualify for a senior discount. Add in AARP, AAA, military, professional, or employee membership discounts and these add up to additional savings, even if your spouse qualifies on account of age.
- Check the classifieds for gently used equipment, furniture, estate pieces, auctions, secondhand stores, warehouse clubs, and garage or moving sales. Proceed with caution when purchasing anything electronic or delicate (such as camera equipment, computers, or printers).
- Configure your own furniture (as in earlier example) or rehab an unfinished or used piece. Never pay full price in a retail showroom. Floor models and remnants might also suit a budget.
- Understand your telephone plan. These days most plans don't discriminate regarding after-hours calls and faxes. In fact, eFax services allow you to send and receive faxes via the Internet.
- Use second-day services (rather than overnight delivery). An Amazon PRIME membership, if you order enough to justify the cost, pays for itself. Since writers are readers, select slower service and receive a digital credit toward eBooks or videos. Other retailers are rolling out their own reduced shipping plans.
- When Amazon offers you a pantry, home cleaning, cosmetics, or alternative credits, kindly refuse and ask for credits that save on what you need.
- Use self-addressed stamped postcards (with check-off options) rather than envelopes.
- Send finished manuscripts or published clips via email, unless otherwise instructed.
- Recycle shipping boxes (if they are in good shape) but always have a supply of manila envelopes and packaging tape handy.
- Affix postage and mailing labels straight, not haphazardly. Try to type/print an address (with your return address)

rather than handwrite it. Anything hastily assembled becomes a big red flag because media outlets and publishers have unfortunately been the target of suspicious packages.

- Have a stamp that reads "requested material" since this carries more clout past the gatekeepers; only use this when you have indeed made contact with your recipient and have been given the go-ahead to submit your work.
- Prepare your own simple tax returns, using software such as TurboTax.
- Use toll-free numbers and free Wi-Fi, saving on data usage. Without a landline, you have no choice but to give out your cell phone number. Don't give it out indiscriminately or you pay for that in constant interruptions when you are in the proverbial concentration or writing zone.
- Purchase office supplies when items are marked down after the back-to-school, fall rush.
- Strike a mutually agreeable arrangement with a vendor and barter services.
- Add an endorsement onto your homeowner's insurance policy. This is the easiest option if you need business coverage but lack enough business income to justify a separate policy.
- Back up all data after every computer shut down. Save lengthy manuscripts on flash drives or lock in a safe deposit box. Remember, your work has monetary value. Create pass phrases rather than passwords that might be more easily breached.

Copyright and Legal Concerns

This brings me to another topic, and now seems as good a time as any to insert this discussion of copyright and symbols.

Beginning writers often feel a burning need to display the copyright symbol so that an editor won't rip off their work. Invariably, new writers often present the copyright notice incorrectly; of course, doing so broadcasts their beginner status, even more glaringly.

Trust me when I say that on any given day, editors are not looking to steal a writer's work. They have so much on their minds amid editorial, art, and advertising department contact, publisher meetings, and telephone calls. They don't wake up pondering, "Gee, what writer will I rip off today?"

Are there unscrupulous editors out there? Possibly. Yet it is so incredibly rare for an editor to risk his job and thousands in legal fees for a magazine manuscript that costs (on average) a few hundred or less for the company to purchase?

If you've created a finished book or extremely unique content—we're *not* talking query letters, magazine or newspaper features, or greeting card captions—then apply for a formal copyright. Your project had better warrant the trouble and expense. Call the Copyright Office toll-free 1-877-476-0778 or (202) 707-3000 for technical support, but if you log on to https://www.copyright.gov/registration/, you'll find a wealth of information on registering copyrights that may eliminate the need for telephone assistance.

To register a book, for instance, you must fill out and send the Copyright Form TX, a check with the current registration fee, and nonreturnable copies of the to-be-registered work to the Library of Congress. Fees vary, but as of this writing, to register one work by a single author, it costs $35; otherwise, online registration costs $55.

Under the Copyright Act (Title 17 of the U.S. code), as of March 1, 1989, copyright exists by mere fact that someone created the work, and not by whether notice has been posted. Notices are no longer mandatory as they were prior to March 1989. For work sent to most publishers, you risk branding yourself the amateur if you display the copyright symbol unnecessarily. If you circulate material widely (such as with teaching handouts) displaying the proper notice may prevent possible infringement. Use your best judgment.

While registration is not required for copyright to exist, it's necessary to a successful infringement lawsuit. Most claims, though, are settled out of court.

If you want to cite copyrighted material in your own work, determine if you must seek formal permission from the copyright holder. If you're excerpting a very small fraction of the work, you may not need to seek a formal permission provided you quote accurately and cite any sources.

You must judge the ratio of work to excerpt; hence, one line from a poem is substantial whereas one sentence out of a sizeable non-fiction book, properly cited, could be seen as an ordinary quote, extending the research or discussion of a topic, or simply providing publicity. You are always safer with the formal permission. Some publishers require these and insist upon signed releases if you are writing about identifiable people.

The doctrine of "fair use" allows for copyrighted material to be cited for research, teaching, news reporting, criticism, limited publicity, and similar purposes. We've seen news headlines of people lifting entire passages of another's speech or written work, claiming it as their own.

Other writers succumb to sloppy habits of not using quotation marks to cite passages generated by another author. This is plagiarism, stealing another writer's work, including a replication of vivid detail and sequence of thought, and it's patently ridiculous. Follow the prescribed procedures of seeking permission, quoting, and citing your sources legally and ethically.

Many authors will be grateful for the publicity; however, they will be incensed if you claim their work as your own. Never—ever—fabricate interviews and quoted passages. Those who yearn to invent fiction should concentrate on novels.

For books, most standard contracts call for the publisher to apply for the copyright in the author's name. Double-check a book's copyright to find if it's royalty-based or a work-for-hire project, if you see that the publisher owns the copyright.

Any serious journalist should have a working knowledge of libel, which refers to printed or broadcast communication where a statement injures reputation, holding someone else up to hatred or ridicule, contempt, ostracism, extreme anguish and humiliation. Publishers often insist upon signed releases when you incorporate privileged details about private individuals.

Of course, truth is the best defense against libel, but writers don't need to invite hassles. That is why when wannabe novelists ask if they can portray a character based upon someone in real life, they are best served if they combine traits from many sources to create an entirely unique character.

Those who write non-fiction, based upon their business or healthcare experience must change names, demographic details, and any other identifying circumstances. Building a composite example of multiple cases or people is the safest and best way to incorporate real-life experience into written account. Always incorporate a disclaimer into the beginning of books or in some other projects stating that you have changed identifying details.

The supposed victim of any libel claim must prove actual economic damage or mental anguish. It is also significant whether the alleged assault took place against a private or public person. People who have thrust themselves into the public arena must prove malice or that the journalist made the statement with a reckless disregard for the truth. It is somewhat different for private persons, but the bottom line here remains—get your facts entirely straight—and consult a lawyer if in doubt.

Classes, Conferences & Writers Residencies

I was encouraged to see that half of those I polled about their writing lives felt that networking and socializing with other writers was well worth the expense. Thirty-six percent of those surveyed reported that volunteering to assist other writers brought relationship and altruistic rewards their way.

By far the best ways to go about socializing also coincides with the education writers receive by attending classes, workshops, lectures, and writer's conferences. Some may even opt for a writer's residency, out of their own geographic area, to bolster their professional development.

Classes and workshops delve into craft, which writers work to improve. Each year, read a few how-to books, those that advance your writing skill. When you join writing associations, attend monthly meetings or critique groups, participate in interactive webinars, you keep in touch with the writing world.

Writer's conferences provide outstanding opportunities to network, providing a full day, sometimes more, of instruction regarding craft and sessions relating to sales, pitches and querying, social media, marketing, cheerleading and inspiration. Some allow meetings with agents and editors. I have spoken at conferences about boosting income, the creative spirit, and incorporating accurate human behavior into one's writing.

Writer's residencies or retreats go a few steps further. This is a quiet colony for writers to do their own work, surrounded by others laboring over the same. The length of stay spans two weeks in some cases to several months. Workshops and social events for networking often come with the territory.

A few are competitive; others have particular missions or philosophies. Of course, if you're spending days on end with other artists and writers the costs go with it. Be selective about what recharges you in terms of scenery and camaraderie.

If you've never been to a writer's conference, it's high time you commit to attending one. You'll leave with copious new ideas and the infectious spirit of other writers. Not to mention that for many, mere attendance signals a thrill deep in their souls that now they really do identify as a bona fide writer. For others, it can literally spark the desire for a vocation, a side gig, or an encore career in retirement.

Find a conference near you through Internet searches, writing magazines, word of mouth referral, or the social media of writing groups. When I attend such events, I always walk away charged up, even if I was hired to do a fraction of that charging.

Conferences generally focus more on lecture and some interaction with attendees whereas workshops may indeed be more hands on. They market through social media with links to see the program and the speaker profiles before you register.

According to a feature in *The Writer* (February 2018), cardinal rules of good conferences include payment of the presenters, plus something that defines the experience as unique for take-away value. What makes a conference unique? Well, perhaps its setting, size, commitment to certain evergreen topics or the fact that it reflects current trends in writing education.

Some conferences enjoy being large; others keep it small, personal, and attendees like that approach and how it feels.

If your budget is tight, avoid spanning multiple days because it will necessitate overnight hotel stays. Having said that, if you have family or friends in the area and can combine with other work activities, go for those conferences in other parts of your region or across the country for that matter.

The American Society of Journalists and Authors (ASJA) conferences have taken place for the past seventy years for non-fiction writers. Its New York conference taps top editors, agents, and freelance talent including top-name keynote speakers. If staying in such a large city seems pricey for your budget, ASJA also holds regional conferences.

Writer's Digest also hosts an annual event encompassing many genres and appealing to a broad base of writers. It, too, has been held in New York City.

One of the best ways to learn is helping others. Work the registration table, be a greeter or room monitor. Well before the event, stuff folders or tote bags. I guarantee you'll get to know other established writers and creative professionals.

These folks will welcome any specialized, tangible help you can render. Do you know how to write a press release? Design the program for the print shop? Prepare a grant proposal for additional funding?

Volunteering to help at events can also lower attendance costs. If you want to travel to out-of-town venues, find another writing friend willing to share the drive and hotel room.

By all means, go to a conference prepared with at least one letter-sized pad of paper and pens. Having helped to organize conferences, I chuckle at some of the suggestions. Most are terrific and spot-on. One respondent thought it best that we supply said implements and paper on site. Since we strive to keep everyone's costs down, we rather expect that writers anticipate taking notes at a, ahem, writing conference.

Yes, bring those necessities as well as a tote bag, small, refillable bottle of water (though some conferences provide these), reading glasses, business cards for networking, and a pouch or re-sealable bag to collect other people's cards. Throat lozenges, tissues, and a small bottle of hand sanitizer are handy to have along with anything else necessary for a long day away from home or the office.

If the conference you attend allows you to present or submit work to a reviewer, be sure to follow the guidelines. Conference committees lament the latecomer who hands in a lengthy manuscript or sample chapters after the published deadline.

In fact, being one of the early submissions may mean a more leisurely, less rushed review of your material. This creates a win-win for all concerned.

When your manuscript receives its review, remember that the feedback represents one informed opinion. Try not to be put off or discouraged if it isn't glowing. Therein lies having those realistic expectations about this field. The best work stems from revision. Period.

As I stated earlier, find morsels of truth and take-away value from the entire conference and manuscript review process, if the event includes this feature.

Pulling It All Together

Accept that to succeed you must sacrifice leisure time to stay employed, earning income and that publishing operates far slower than we might like.

In the next chapter, I'll address how there is no such thing as a former client. Marketing, even in subtle ways, will often turn dormant clients into current, paying ones.

Nine

Marketing Grows a Business

Consumers do not buy products.
They buy product benefits.
— David Ogilvy, advertising tycoon

If you wait until you must market yourself or your writing business, you have waited way too long. Marketing is an ever-evolving pursuit. Sure, there will be times when actually executing the projects you've worked diligently to acquire will take priority, and they should. Too many small businesses and independent professionals—you as a writer fit into either or both category—view marketing as a necessary evil. Simply not so.

Building a Portfolio of Samples and Clips

One main difference between those writers who see their names in print and those who do not comes down to self-promotion. In all fairness, it may also be accountable to hiding one's work in the desk drawer. That won't boost your bank account either. You need action.

Just as you must create quality material and effectively sell it to feel gratified and earn the monetary validation you seek, so too, you must be your own cheerleader for your accomplishments.

Does that sound self-absorbed? Not exactly. As I discussed in bragging rights, there's nothing wrong with alerting others that your work is out there. In fact—highlight here—you must.

Clips (short for clippings or tear sheets) prove that you are published. This is merely an industry term for effective photocopies—effective being the operative word. You should not just slap any old clipping onto a photocopier and pray it comes out clear and straight. Master the art of a simple graphic paste-up and/or be sure to scan carefully and trim the image if you must.

Try to obtain at least one original copy of your published work, more if you can snag them. Cut out the masthead. If too large (such as a daily newspaper), find a small version inside, along with a publication date. With the Internet and Google Images, you should find a publication logo with relative ease, download it, and manipulate it to the size that fits your clipping.

Date everything you clip, even material for your research files. Have you ever referred to some earlier clipping and had no clue how dated the research was? Exactly. Editors desire more current samples of your work, and the date provides this.

Paste the publication's masthead, the publication date, along with your clipping onto a standard sheet of paper (letter not legal size). If necessary, reduce it to fit this size page.

No masthead? Then type the publication's name and date. Use the photo lightness/darkness command to create a pleasing photocopy. Neatness counts. Correction fluid helps to disguise any specks or lines that don't belong.

Published clips sell you and your ability to write. Writers used to mail or fax these to editors. Repeat work for the same clients or publications creates an even more positive impression.

Online links to your work direct editors to websites where your work has been published. Here's the rub, however. What happens when the link no longer exists?

Exactly. You are out of luck and some editor who clicks on it to see proof of your being published is now disappointed. Back to why I advocate building a file with physical clippings. Scan them for a digital set. If you submit a non-fiction book proposal and need these as part of that effort, you will have them.

Rarely do writers have to present binders with physical specimens of their writing unless an in-person interview results. If you do need to, be sure that your portfolio doesn't shout school supply. Make it a professional looking binder.

Drive More Business Your Way

One key to remaining successful as a writer, particularly a self-employed one, is to keep tabs on trends, the social climate, and technological advances. When some craze or a new gadget captures people's collective attention, ask yourself what looms ahead? Where might problems arise?

That's not to be pessimistic, but a lot of journalism is problem-to-solution-focused. Take smartphones. They are so customary today, but when they first launched, did parents stop to consider that their pre-teen or adolescent kids might get into trouble with what we now call sexting? That's only one example, but if you can train your mind to think forward, you will have some advantages over your contemporaries who do not.

A job well done will always keep clients calling you next time they need editorial content, a business project, a promotion campaign or whatever it is that you write. In my survey to colleagues, I also asked how writers used their time during slow spells or recessionary periods. Thirty-six percent responded that they would spend more time working on longer-length projects that they had put off. Twenty-two percent would enter a new writing arena that they previously have not attempted.

Yet the best answer: twenty-two percent didn't need to stress over the down times because they had routinely networked and marketed themselves. These folks rarely experienced a lack of income due to less demand for their services. As you may have gleaned, marketing over time equates to a lot more income security and fewer monetary worries. When editor or client calls drop off, use your time wisely to:

- Take a fresh look at the business profile you market
- Consider a business graphic—other than a quill pen—to explain your work visually
- Refresh stationery, business cards, and email signatures
- Contact dormant or prospective clients to boost referrals
- Update social media and analyze what draws interest
- Get listed on other referral sites or bases
- Propose talks to community, PTA or library groups
- Join in online with LinkedIn, Facebook, or Yahoo groups
- Revamp your website; monetize it to sell products

No editor or company can hire you if the key decision makers don't know you exist or aren't aware of your skills. Market yourself as you wish to be perceived, as either a generalist or specialist. The best vehicle to advertise, display and promote what you do as a writer remains a custom website.

Sample Author Websites

When you're a writer in the business of attracting clients and selling your work, you need an Internet presence and social media sites.

Irene Panke Hopkins, a West Coast freelance writer and editor, has an impressive website at irenehopkins.com. The graphics, photos and text boxes provide sufficient color to an overall clean, crisp site that's easy to navigate. Along the navigation bar, you'll spot the following buttons: About, My Blog, Portfolio, Client Testimonials, Services & Rates, and a Contact option. I especially liked her portfolio with brief descriptions and because Irene delineates her work with distinct categories.

Don Sadler, a Georgia-based business and financial writer, keeps his web presence very simple and sleek at donsadlerwriter.com. Upon a white background, Sadler has navigation prompts for Home page, Blog, About, Samples, Clients, Testimonials, and Contact. To the right, there's a Sign Up for his monthly newsletter, Contact Info and Recent Posts.

On the site of comedian, writer and speech coach Steve Calechman, he features Articles and News, a Contact section in the middle with information about his Next Show, an option to click on his full calendar of stand-up performances, and another option to Be on My Mailing List. View his site at stevecalechman.com. Other tabs along the navigation bar include Home, Comedy, Writing, Speech Coaching, and a Search icon.

Sharon Naylor writes feature articles and books about the wedding industry. Her webpage at sharonnaylor.net features elegant script for her name and a photo section with images that crawl. She offers a four-line biography or explanation of her site and then a stylish Read More tab. Further down her page, you can see each book with a button to Learn More and then check out her most recent blogs with similar options below each. At the very bottom, Sharon has icons for Facebook, Twitter, Instagram and LinkedIn on the left, a Search My Site on the right.

Given the web development credits for these various author websites, each invests in their online presence. Key elements to pay attention to on the site you develop include listing your qualifications, past work, writing samples, any specialization that you have, as well as testimonials.

Some writers balk at listing their rates. I understand that hesitancy, but if you don't wish for the world to see what you earn, then have some means or ask for the potential client to obtain a quote. In fact, that "ask" is vital in leading people to your services. Write with search engine optimization (SEO) in mind so that your site will be discoverable. A future book will highlight more of this skill and the practices associated with online writing.

Tooting Your Own Talents

Beyond a web presence, word of mouth begins with yours. Tell everyone you are a writer. Key people—those who have hired you in the past or are prime prospects for doing so in the future—should know when you make news, win awards, give speeches, TV or radio interviews, and publish books or articles.

"My biggest mistake early on was in figuring my output would speak for itself and the work would follow," Steve Calechman admits. "What I've learned is that you have to let people know that you exist and that you want to work for them." He refers to this as schmoozing and good old hanging out.

"It doesn't have to be egregious," Steve concludes, "but you have to show an enthusiasm for what you do for the ultimate purpose of building relationships, having people not only think of you and your work, but also take your calls."

What are the best practices around doing this self-promotion? How do you get others to say positive comments about your work? As Steve, and other professionals I've interviewed suggest, you ask. You share.

If you're truly creative and have the time, send a newsletter or some brief brochure. Most word processing programs already have templates that make this very easy and less time consuming than creating a newsletter from scratch.

You'll find when you seek out speaking engagements that many groups may not have budgets. Speaking gratis, simply for the promotional value, may bring extra income in the form of new business or book sales. Leave nothing to chance. Write the introduction for any hosts introducing you. In fact, with every submission to a commercial publisher, craft your own bio. Control what image you present.

The 80/20 rule applies to all businesspeople, including writers. You will find that eighty percent of your business comes from twenty percent of your clients (editors, too). So, keep those folks happy. It's great to have not only the income but also the routine of working with the same clients. The convenience has a flip side, of course. Lose two clients and that's substantial.

Diversification and writing for new markets can help writers survive a tough economy. The more markets or editors you query, the better your odds of always having steady work. When you've successfully completed a job, ask satisfied clients for their endorsement, even if in a quick e-mail.

Ask for quantified results. For instance, if your clients can say that sales of products improved by forty percent, largely because of a marketing publication you designed, that is concrete and convincing evidence as a testimonial. Use it to attract future work.

Social Media Matters

I have purposely woven marketing throughout this book. Whether through social media, website development, or word of mouth sales, it's all in the realm of marketing.

Regardless of your being a seasoned pro or just building a list of initial writing clients, take every available opportunity to market your writing services. Pick up additional guidance and tips at conferences or workshops. Read writing magazines, blogs and books that provide this advice. Continue with this series.

In our digital age and armed with additional social media tools, some think that they can plunge right in, garner fans, sell tons of books, and field incoming client calls. Not so fast. You have choices to make. Don't join a forum or platform because someone else loves it. Choose two platforms, possibly three, that you can commit time to and feel comfortable using.

I highly recommend *The Essential Social Media Marketing Handbook* by Gail Z. Martin with its recurring themes of thinking through consequences of social engagement and giving first to communities you join. I covered some of this earlier. "Details made public cannot be taken back," Martin reminds. Safety issues and other people's privacy remain at risk if you act hastily.

The same goes for your frustrations in social media snags. *Overcoming Passive-Aggression* has the subtitle *How to Stop Hidden Anger from Spoiling Your Relationships, Career and Happiness.* Losing your composure or spewing thinly veiled digs in awkward tweets or online rants you later regret or others will resent blemishes your credibility. And, unless you've been camped in the woods for much of the past few years, you have surely heard about headlines gone viral after someone made an off-the-cuff remark. Some of this has ended careers.

This doesn't mean that you should stay silent. Introverts may need to nudge themselves to share bits and pieces of their inspiration, feelings, and activities to make themselves personable; extroverts might need to pull back from the sheer number of status updates. Provide too much detail and your fans won't enjoy any curiosity or mystery about the writing process. When tempted to vent, lift those fingers from your keyboard. Wait a day (or three) and revisit the matter.

Other Marketing Avenues

People build connections with other humans, as evidenced by the popularity of personal testimonials and videos, talking directly to fans in thirty- to sixty-second videos to draw attention. This also feeds the entertainment-thirsty algorithms. "You don't have to be a rock star, supermodel or professional actor," Gail Martin writes. "Be yourself, provide value. Let people get to know you."

I have heard a similar version of this advice from Laura Reeth, who handles the social media for Maryland novelist Nora Roberts/J.D. Robb. I've gotten to know Laura from conferences I've attended and organized. Video is indeed where it's at these days. Visit social media pages to see how other writers do this. Try the approach for yourself and witness whether the reach extends farther than text or graphic posts.

Public relations and visual images educate and engage. Advertising can complement. Done too heavily, it builds walls akin to the telemarketer calling during the dinner hour. That's why many writers use data science to their advantage online.

The big players, including but not limited to Amazon, Facebook and Google, track online movements. When pop-up ads for products searched for yesterday appear today, it's admittedly a little creepy but this is the digital world we live in.

Be a part of it or abstain at your own potential peril. Organic reach, where Facebook and other platforms began, only gets so far today. Thanks to ever-changing, complicated algorithms, you may need to adapt repeatedly to reach your ideal readers.

Whatever you do, Gail Martin advises that you cultivate connections, online and offline, with primary influencers. Visibility begets visibility, she writes. Influencers are those who have published widely, knowing more than you do. If they are a part of what Martin calls "your tribe," others notice.

Even if you're not a book author, it's a good idea to promote qualified traffic (readers who are your target audience) to your social media, website and email signup list.

Never underestimate the power of a good list. It's the digital equivalent of a direct mail campaign. "A highly targeted list for traditional paper-based mailings shouldn't be overlooked," says Leslie Walker, a visiting professor of digital innovation at the University of Maryland's Philip Merrill College of Journalism. "I believe printed mailings may be old fashioned, but they increasingly stand out as the world continues to go electronic."

Indeed, these campaigns can be worthwhile investments for events, book launches, and other projects we will learn about later in this book series. Perhaps a balance of electronic mail, with the help of Constant Contact, Mail Chimp or other services, and traditional direct mail promotion has a place in your marketing strategy.

Ten

Bank Money, Savor the Rewards

*If you're walking down the right path and you're willing
to keep walking, eventually you'll make progress.*
— Barack Obama, 44th US President

We have come to the end of the path, at least with this book. I will intentionally keep this chapter concise and fun, but before we part, there are a few last-minute mentions to help you meet with success and profit.

Networking aids most everyone, and of course, writers. When you undertake a side gig, decide to leave a full-time job, or commit to an encore career, I find it wise to talk with other professionals who have gone before you. Sometimes, we are tempted to surround ourselves only with likeminded people, and there's good reason at times for doing this. Not here.

Talk to as many writers as you can. So what if you don't intend to write humor or greeting cards? No matter if you have no desire to write a poem, short story, novel, picture book, or magazine feature, meet those who are willing to share what motivated them, how it's gone for them, their triumphs, and worst days. Find a group of writers on Meetup.com if you can't discover them anywhere else.

Ask others what they would do over again? Find out what strategies they use to set aside emergency money, how many months they saved up before going it alone, and how they fund important insurances most employees receive as part of their benefit packages.

Are they willing to give a range of their rates or financial picture? Without being too inquisitive, ask the range of remuneration they receive and possibly why they stopped writing in certain areas or decided to add or undertake others.

Remember: you may hear lots of regrets and stories of sunken dreams. Anyone new to an endeavor charts a course and learns from it. Make it a point to override dashed hopes and possible horror stories with positivity. Put a bit more emphasis in your memory bank on those who sailed to success for this reason and replicate their best business practices into your own new habits.

Business Plans

When I was in graduate school, I took a very useful one-credit course on having a private practice. As a project, we wrote a business plan. I found this exercise to be very useful, and I'm pleased to say that I have lived up to that plan in my career as a mental health therapist.

This exercise forced me to reflect upon my former career where I worked out of necessity adding income as a freelancer, but then just allowed various opportunities to evolve. It does seem, in hindsight, that I flew by the seat of my pants (pantzer vs. plotter approach) or the needs of my bank account and family circumstances. Sometimes one has to. Life and priorities prevail but carve out time to journal and type these items below.

A basic business plan contains an overview of your goals, a mission statement, and description. What is it you set out to do? What are your strengths? Incorporate these.

Next, it looks at your target market or clientele. Is it broad enough to meet the financial goals that you have in your personal life? Look at your competition and what differentiates you as a writer or small business person. Why should clients choose you over anyone else, in other words?

How will you manage time and any help that you need? What is that assistance? If you write books, you will need to budget for editing, cover design and the like, should you decide to Indie publish. If you tackle tasks yourself, build in and budget that time, doubling what you expect, especially if you're new to tasks.

If small business projects like on-hold messages are your style, what's your game plan to meet the decision makers and get your work before them?

What is your financial outlook? How will you market your services and products such as books?

Finally, and usually at the end of this, brainstorm for business names. Resist the urge to fall in love with the first idea that pops into your mind. Run it past some trusted friends or colleagues.

Write a one-page, no more than a two-page, summary. It helps when you must craft an elevator speech should you have to explain your concept or apply for financing. It's wise to have a confidentiality agreement, asking those who review this plan to sign it upfront before you have disclosed your intentions.

Service Corps of Retired Executives, otherwise known as SCORE (www.score.org), has a business plan that you can download. It's very detailed and perhaps way more than the average writer needs. However, it gives you plenty to think about, and if your business extends to publishing others, hiring help, and having a lot of inventory, it may be well worth a look. Also, consult the resource section.

Making $$ Doing What You Enjoy

I am very hopeful that this book has boosted your productivity, your professional sights, and your self-image, perhaps yielding a few more sales if you're self-employed. The best-case scenario: You commit creative energies that you never knew you had to try some of the new writing approaches or jobs out of the pages you have just read. I assure you that in the books that follow in my series, there will be plenty more ideas.

Will you enjoy all of these writing paths? That would be ideal, but there is a reason that jobs are called work. I'll bet that those of you who began writing for the heck of it or because it was an artistic, fun outlet soon learned upon revision, spelling and grammar checks, not to mention at deadline or promotion phases that your once sought-after hours tapping fingers upon the keyboard now seemed so much more deliberate and serious.

We spend an inordinate amount of our days in the pursuit of a job, career, and income. In my opinion, a day can't get much better when you start and end it pursuing a passion that you love.

Even if you must spend your days in another kind of toil or with other job-related tasks, you can feel the same fulfillment as a part-time writer.

Success Stories

Celebrity artist Andy Warhol once claimed, "Making money is art and working is art and good business is the best art."

What's more Robert Kiyosaki, a best-selling author of financial books, says, "A wealthy person is simply someone who has learned how to make money when they're not working."

So true! While many of the projects you read about in this book earn you a paycheck each time you create, ultimately if you broaden your base to books or other writing with a fan or subscription base, you may indeed rake in the profits while you golf, swim, or even sleep!

That does not mean you should opt to give away your day job. Not yet, anyway. I added a second career being a mental health clinician after decades as a writer. Then, I missed writing enough to return to the keyboard and now combine the two careers. I don't think I'm ever idle enough to be bored, just ask my family.

Writing is one of those endeavors that lends itself to be an ideal encore career for many, especially those who have leveraged twenty to forty years in another field. I cannot begin to tell you how many of my former students and readers of prior writing books fit this profile. Keep reading for links provided by the American Association of Retired Persons (AARP), a non-profit interest group focused upon living well after retirement.

Examples of Career Transitions

"My father said writing was a nice hobby, not something you could make money at," said Tess Gerritsen, author of the TNT Rizzoli/Isles series, among dozens of published titles. Gerritsen is the child of a Chinese immigrant and a Chinese-American seafood chef.

While Tess dreamed of being a writer, her family clearly had its reservations. Thus, she became a physician. I had the opportunity to meet Tess and hear her story and her insights at a writing conference.

She began writing her first novel in the on-call room as an intern. Now *that* is dedication. I'd be fast asleep. Years later while on maternity leave, she submitted a short story to a contest, won first prize, and like many writers that fueled her onward. Two "practice" unpublished novels later, she sold *Call After Midnight* to Harlequin Intrigue in 1986.

For the next ten years she wrote for this imprint and Harper Paperbacks until in 1996, she branched into writing medical thrillers. *Harvest,* her first hardcover novel debuted on the *New York Times* bestseller list. It wasn't the first and only time she made that distinction.

Such inspiration exists everywhere, in all genres, and so do the myriad of reasons to write.

Janet Bodnar began her journalistic career decades ago at *The Providence Journal* and *The Washington Post* before joining *Kiplinger Personal Finance* magazine. She has a master's degree from Columbia University, and while there, was a fellow in business/economics journalism.

At Kiplinger's, Janet worked as a writer and subsequently rose to the top in the editorial ranks. She was recognized by *Folio* as one of the Top Women in Media and is nationally regarded for expertise in the realm of children and family financial matters.

In 2017, Janet stepped down, so to speak since the masthead still lists her as editor at large. With well-deserved time to herself, she continues to write a monthly column for the magazine.

You can see in both of these fiction and non-fiction examples that transition can come easily. That's not always the case, but something you may have more control over than you might think.

The Gig Economy

The Washington Post devoted a section of the paper to a grad guide in May 2017. In a column headlined "Need to pay off debt? Put your side hustle front and center," David Carlson, the writer, encouraged recent graduates to get ahead of their financial responsibilities by creating another way to make money. He dubbed it a side hustle, and yes, freelance writing was one of those areas he mentioned.

Months later, *Money* magazine featured "101 Ways to Make $1,000" (December 2017), and wouldn't you know that getting a gig, including becoming a freelance copywriter, website designer or graphic artist was very much encouraged.

Rest assured, there is a place for you in the ranks of publishing and print. Never before has the world been so information-driven, demanding news instantly, the second after it occurs. Yet, with all that jockeys for our precious time, people want their information delivered succinctly with a focus on how to become healthier, wealthier, wiser, more successful, more popular, or just plain happier. Much depends upon your qualifications, talent, the time you can devote to your craft, and plain old luck. However, the sky is the limit.

If monetary rewards are not your primary or secondary priorities, so be it. I hope you will remain with this series because you will likely glean tips to make you more successful.

The more you write, the better a writer you'll become. With each query letter, pitch, or submission to editors, companies and clients, the more convincing your pitches and sales become. Eventually, the results add up. Often, avocations become vocations. Funny how that happens!

Your publishing road may be a high-speed expressway to a six-figure income, or it may be that side hustle that nets you just enough money to sleep better at night, stash away some extra funds or finance a wonderful vacation.

Stephen Hawking, a best-selling author, has been quoted as saying that "I first had the idea of writing a popular book about the universe in 1982. My intention was partly to earn money to pay my daughter's school fees." I think you'll agree he probably paid that many times over through his writing successes.

The same goes for J.K. Rowling who has said, "Rock bottom became the solid foundation on which I rebuilt my life." Joseph Heller said, "I wanted to be a writer because I felt I had a gift, and I really wanted to make money and have some kind of status."

All of these reasons are perfectly fine and to be respected. Another irony may also occur. While writing may start as a hobby, then turn monetary, much like a job, you might actually enjoy it...or delight in its satisfying needs that your day job or career does not. Then, there's no turning back.

People used to ask Elmore Leonard why he was still writing books. It took him aback as if "I'm still only writing to make money and as soon as I have enough I'll quit and go fishing? I like to write books," he said. "It's the most satisfying thing I do."

Keep the Creative Embers Alive

Remember when I said that I have never met a dedicated writer who is not concurrently an avid reader. That's because reading and listening to audio books helps a writer to broaden vocabulary, tune in to new techniques, and develop style. Seeing proper grammar and punctuation also reinforces this very necessary part of the craft as well.

Your life is busy and so is mine. Most writers I know read using a variety of platforms available, including Audible and Hoopla for auditory learners; Kindle, Nook, Flipboard, Overdrive and Libby gadget Apps for books or news reporting.

To focus their concentration, writers should try the morning pages, ala Julia Cameron and her seminal book *The Artist's Way*. They might sequester themselves for hours alone or use soothing music or white noise in the background. Simply Noise is one such white noise App.

Most creative people appreciate comedy because it's helpful to their work. You live in the same world as I do so…it's sanity saving. I challenge you to embrace comedy even more. Tune into monologues, comedy channels, and standup performances to absorb these techniques.

Finally, relax with or without the popcorn to be motivated by the reel press. Yes, that was purposeful, not a misspelling. On-screen portrayals have inspired me, perhaps you as well. I grew up with *The Mary Tyler Moore Show* and then decades later watched *Murphy Brown* on television.

Were you a *30 Rock* fan or did you watch *Newsroom* or *Sports Night*? Did you catch the PBS Frontline series called *News Wars?*

This later three-part series outlined the effects of the Internet revolution, the pressure for profits, changing media values, first-amendment and national security challenges, controversies, and legal battles. Learn from more than fifty sources interviewed and read about the series at pbs.org.

Whenever you question why your energies go where they do, watch a good documentary or flick to renew the commitment to telling your story, reporting information, or even to the first amendment most writers hold in the highest regard.

20 Major Films to Nurture Your Inner Journalist

- *Citizen Kane* (1941)
- *All the President's Men* (1976)
- *The Killing Fields* (1984)
- *Broadcast News* (1987)
- *Misery* (1990)
- *The Pelican Brief* (1993)
- *The Paper* (1994)
- *Up Close & Personal* (1996)
- *One Fine Day* (1996)
- *The Insider* (1999)
- *The Adaptation* (2002)
- *Beyond Borders* (2003)
- *Shattered Glass* (2003)
- *Good Night, and Good Luck* (2005)
- *Frost/Nixon* (2008)
- *Page One* (2011)
- *Spotlight* (2015)
- *Money Monster* (2016)
- *Mark Felt: Man Who Brought Down the White House* (2017)
- *The Post* (2017)

Rushed into development by director Steven Spielberg and miraculously put before reviewers a mere nine months after Spielberg had the script in hand, *The Post* depicts the challenges that writers, publishers, and courts face. There's a bravery element to this movie coupled with a strong woman (publisher Katharine Graham) finding her voice and assertively showing it on screen.

Each movie shows a driving focus to uncover facts, report news, following journalistic values and the commitment to one's job. *The Killing Fields* and *The Post* drive home disturbing realities such as genocide and war. A few films feature the broadcast industry where words and image both matter.

Some are comedic, others terrorizing. *Misery* and *The Adaptation* show writers creating…or trying to. *Page One* is a documentary about the evolving way people receive information. Several cast our attention upon newspaper investigative reporting.

See if your picks parallel mine. There are other films for sure, but this list I hope keeps you thinking of your craft and inspired.

What's Your Path?

We are at the end of our journey. You have pondered numerous approaches and concepts here. I thank you for taking this time with me as we explored what has influenced, inspired, and created productive and often highly-acclaimed writers.

Afraid you're not up to the challenge? You are. Concerned you won't have enough time to do it all? You won't. Leary of making a few mistakes along the way? You will.

Unlike brain surgery, rocket science, and maybe having two strikes at the end of the ninth inning, you get more than one chance to get things right…or write! The best work stems from revision. Plenty of it. There's no time like the present, as well as tomorrow, and the next day.

Revisit the goals or curiosities you jotted down, as prompted, in the first chapter. Have these changed? Has your determination, after reading these pages?

One last mental reframe: If you don't choose to write about what you know—or want to know—someone else will. Focus on what you can offer. Be that writer. Reap the recognition, possible job promotions, income advantages, and a few other perks of the writing life, along the way.

Shore Thing Publishing
PROOF COPY

RESOURCES AND READING

Chapter One: Paths to Different Profits

R. Gillett, "From Welfare to One of the World's Wealthiest Women—the Incredible Rags-to-Riches Story of J.K. Rowling," *Business Insider*, May 18, 2015.

K. Dickerson, "The Surprising Story of How Andy Weir's Self-Published Book 'The Martian' topped Best-Seller Lists & Got Movie Deal," *Business Insider*, June 22, 2015.

Pew Research Center, "State of the News Media 2016," June 15, 2016

M. Coker, "10 Self-Publishing Trends to Watch," *Publisher's Weekly*, July 22, 2016.

J. Milliot, "Adult Nonfiction Stayed Hot in 2016," *Publisher's Weekly*, Jan. 13, 2017.

P. Anderson, "Industry Notes: US Ebook Sales Slightly Up in May," *Publishing Perspectives*, September 29, 2017.

Writer's Market 2018: The Most Trusted Guide to Getting Published, 97th Edition (Cincinnati, OH: Writer's Digest Books, 2017).

Recommended Periodicals: *Publisher's Weekly, Library Journal, Writer's Digest, The Writer, Poets & Writers*

Chapter Two: Show Me the Money

O*Net OnLine, accessed February 16, 2018, https://www.onetonline.org.

D. Hill, "Keeping Tabs on Who Pays Writers," accessed February 16, 2018, https://nwu.org/keeping-tabs-on-who-pays-writers/.

Freelance Isn't Free Act, accessed February 16, 2018, https://www1.nyc.gov/site/dca/about/freelance-isnt-free-act.page.

S. Horowitz, "Freelance Isn't Free and the Future of Freelancing," accessed Feb. 16, 2018, https://blog.freelancersunion.org/2016/10/28/sara-freelance-isnt-free-act/.

IRS Small Business Week Tax Tip 2017-04, May 3, 2017, https://www.irs.gov/newsroom/hobby-or-business-irs-offers-tips-to-decide.

Recommended Organizations: Author's Guild, Society for Technical Communicators, American Booksellers Association, Editorial Freelancers Association, Freelance Writers Union. See others throughout this resource section.

Chapter Three: Journalism Basics

J.C. Blumenthal, *English 3200* (Boston, MA: Cengage Learning, 1994).

K. Spisak, *Get a Grip on Your Grammar* (Wayne: NJ: Career Press, 2017).

Grammarly App, accessed February 16, 2018, https://www.grammarly.com.

Recommended Reading:
S. King, *On Writing: A Memoir of the Craft*, Anniversary Edition (New York: Scribner, 2010).

W. Zinsser, *On Writing Well: The Classic Guide to Writing Nonfiction*, 30th Anniversary Edition (New York: Harper Collins, 2006).

W. Strunk and E.B. White, *The Elements of Style* (Boston: Allyn & Bacon, 2000).

Chapter Four: Bank Boosting Brief Work

N. Schuman and B.J. Nadler, *1,001 Phrases You Need to Get a Job* (Boston: Adams Media, 2012).

S. Bennett, *The Elements of Résumé Style: Essential Rules for Writing Résumés and Cover Letters That Work*, 2nd Edition (New York: AMACOM, 2015).

K. Bahler, "What Your Résumé Should Look Like in 2018," *MONEY*, March 2018.

USA TODAY Snapshots, accessed Feb. 16, 2018, https://www.usatoday.com/picture-gallery/news/2015/04/07/usa-today-snapshots/6340793/.

Chapter Five: Sentimental Payday

J. Vejnoska, "1.6 Billion Reasons Christmas Cards Aren't Going Away Anytime Soon," *Atlanta Journal-Constitution*, Atlanta Life, December 21, 2016.

USA TODAY Snapshots, accessed Feb. 16, 2018, https://www.usatoday.com/picture-gallery/news/2015/04/07/usa-today-snapshots/6340793/.

J. Smith, "Here's What It's Like to Be One of the 24 Greeting Card Writers at Hallmark," *Business Insider*, February 12, 2016.

Poet's Market 2018: The Most Trusted Guide for Publishing Poetry, 31st Edition (Cincinnati, OH: Writer's Digest Books, 2017).

Recommended Organizations: Greeting Card Association, The Greeting Card Association in the United Kingdom

Chapter Six: Money Is a Joke

L.H. Oberlin and T. Murphy, *Overcoming Passive-Aggression: How to Stop Hidden Anger from Spoiling Your Relationships, Career, and Happiness* (Boston: DaCapo Press, 2016).

M. Shatz and M. Helitzer, "Tickling the Funny Bone," *Writer's Digest*, July 2017.

M. Shatz and M. Helitzer, *Comedy Writing Secrets: The Best-Selling Guide to Writing Funny and Getting Paid for It* (Cincinnati, OH: Writer's Digest Books, 2016).

E. Possey, "Rule of Three Multiplies Effect of Speech Humor," *Austin Business Journal,* October 31, 1999.

E. Barker, "How to Be Funny: Six Essential Ingredients to Humor," *The Week,* March 18, 2014, http://theweek.com/articles/449236/how-funny-6-essential-ingredients-humor.

C. Henshey, "Comedy Writing Secrets: Triple the Funny," There Are No Rules Blog, *Writer's Digest,* February 11, 2016.

G. Perret, J. Medeiros and C. Burnett, *The New Comedy Writing Step by Step: Revised and Updated with Words of Instruction, Encouragement, and Inspiration from Legends of the Comedy Profession* (Fresno, CA: Quill Driver Books, 2007).

Songwriter's Market 40th Edition: Where & How to Market Your Songs (Cincinnati, OH: Writer's Digest Books, 2016).

ZDoggMD: Slightly Funnier Than Placebo, accessed February 16, 2018, http://zdoggmd.com.

Comedy USA, accessed February 16, 2018, http://www.comedyusa.com.

Recommended Reading:
S. Martin, *Born Standing Up: A Comic's Life* (New York: Scribner, 2008).

T. Fey, *Bossypants* (New York: Little Brown, 2011).

M. Sacks, *And Here's the Kicker: Conversations with 21 Top Humor Writers* (New York: Writers House, 2014).

M. Sacks, *Poking a Dead Frog: Conversations with Today's Top Comedy Writers* (New York: Penguin Books, 2014).

Recommended Organizations: National Association of Comedians

Chapter Seven: You've Got This

G. Keller and J. Papasan, *The ONE Thing: The Surprisingly Simple Truth Behind Extraordinary Results* (Austin, TX: Bard Press, 2013).

K.R. Jamison, *Touched with Fire: Manic-Depressive Illness and the Artistic Temperament* (New York: Free Press, 1996).

Brigham and Women's Hospital, Boston, MA, "Irregular Sleeping Patterns Linked to Poorer Academic Performance in College Students," *Science Daily,* June 12, 2017.

Chapter Eight: Solo Success Strategies

B. Berkowitz and P. Clar, "The Health Hazards of Sitting," *The Washington Post,* January 20, 2014.

B.M. Lynch and N. Owen, "Too Much Sitting and Chronic Disease Risk: Steps to Move the Science Forward," *Annals of Internal Medicine,* January 20, 2015.

"Reducing Sedentary Behaviors: Sitting Less and Moving More," Fact Sheet, American College of Sports Medicine, 2011.

Slideshow: 10 Ways to Exercise Hands and Fingers, WebMD, accessed February 16, 2018, https://www.webmd.com/osteoarthritis/ss/slideshow-hand-finger-exercises

IRS Estimated Taxes, accessed Feb., 16, 2018, https://www.irs.gov/businesses/small-businesses-self-employed/estimated-taxes.

"Which Form Should I Use?" Frequently Asked Questions, U.S. Copyright Office, accessed February 16, 2016, https://www.copyright.gov/forms/.

Chapter Nine: Marketing Grows a Business

G.Z. Martin, *The Essential Social Media Marketing Handbook* (Wayne: NJ: Career Press, 2017).

K. Adams, "Social Media for Writers: Which Platforms You Need to Be On, Based on What You Write," *The Writer's Cookbook,* January 26, 2017.

Chapter Ten: Bank Money, Savor Rewards

D. Carlson, "Want to Pay Off Debt and Build Your Finances Faster? Look to the Side Hustle," *The Washington Post,* April 24, 2017

J. Cameron, *The Artist's Way: 25th Anniversary Edition* (New York: Tarcher, 2016)).

A. Adamczyk, K. Mulhere, E. O'Brien and K.A. Renzulli, "101 Ways to Make $1,000/Get a Gig/Make Your Hobby Pay," *MONEY,* December 2017, accessed February 16, 2018, http://time.com/money/page/101-ways-make-1000-more-2018/.

Service Corps of Retired Executives, accessed February 16, 2018, www.score.org.

Small Business Administration, accessed February 16, 2018, www.sba.gov.

"Encore Entrepreneurs," Work & Jobs, Work Life Balance, AARP, June 2016.

Y.S. Lai, "Cardinal Rules of Writer's Conferences," *The Writer,* February, 2018.

FUTURE SERIES TITLES

WRITING TO MAKE MONEY:
FREELANCE & FULL-TIME WORK
to be released Fall 2018

WRITING TO MAKE MONEY:
NOVELS & NON-FICTION BOOKS
to be released 2019

Sign up to receive alerts and news
about the next books
released in this series and others:

www.facebook.com/writingtomakemoney

Order books through links at:
www.loriannoberlin.com/books-articles/

Thank you so very much for spending your reading time with this book.

Please consider rating and leaving a few remarks on online bookstore websites. Rating books and commenting, even if only a few words, supports readership and inspires future projects by authors. ~ Loriann

ABOUT THE AUTHOR

Loriann Hoff Oberlin is a graduate of Westminster College, New Wilmington, PA. She worked in Pittsburgh, PA for eighteen years as a public relations consultant and writer of newspaper and magazine articles as well as greeting cards. Loriann was a regular contributor to bridal, women's, parenting, and airline magazines, among others. She wrote a monthly work-at-home column for the *Pittsburgh Business Times*; taught freelance writing at community colleges, the University of Pittsburgh, and other sites; and was a frequent interview subject of local broadcast and print media. Ms. Oberlin wrote several non-fiction books during this time, including *Writing for Money, Working At Home While The Kids Are There, Too, Surviving Separation and Divorce,* and *The Angry Child.*

Following a move to the Washington, DC area, Ms. Oberlin attended Johns Hopkins University where she earned a master's degree in clinical counseling. She wrote *Overcoming Passive-Aggression* and became a licensed clinical professional counselor. Today, she maintains a private practice with two offices, using cognitive-behavioral therapy and family systems theory to help clients understand and overcome obstacles, set goals, and live according to their values in their personal and professional lives.

Under the pen name Lauren Monroe, Loriann has authored The Maryland Shores women's fiction series, set in the Chesapeake region where she has most recently made her home with her husband and family. Active in advocacy and education for writers, she has volunteered on the planning committee of the Bay to Ocean Writer's Conference for five years, serving as the publicity liaison, in program/speaker planning, and as one of the conference co-coordinators. Reach her at loriannoberlin.com/contact/.

Sign up for her newsletter at facebook.com/writingtomakemoney. Many of her books have an independent social media presence. Keep in touch through websites, including: loriannoberlin.com, laurenmonroenovels.com and facebook.com/lauren.monroe.novels. Loriann has a writing board at www.pinterest.com/novelistlaurenm.

90302831R00078

Made in the USA
Columbia, SC
05 March 2018